PRAYING FOR ANOTHER

Gene A. Getz

While this book is designed for the reader's personal enjoyment and profit, it is also intended for group study. A Leader's Guide with Victor Multiuse Transparency Masters is available from your local bookstore or from the publisher.

VICTOR BOOKS

a division of SP Publications, Inc.
WHEATON. ILLINOIS 60187

Offices also in Fullerton, California • Whitby, Ontario, Canada • Amersham-on-the-Hill, Bucks, England

Recommended Dewey Decimal Classification: 248.3
  Suggested Subject Headings: PRAYER; CHRISTIAN LIFE

Library of Congress Catalog Card Number: 82-60254
ISBN: 0-88207-351-6

VICTOR BOOKS
A division of SP Publications, Inc.
P.O. Box 1825 • Wheaton, Illinois 60187

Contents

A Personal Word

For a number of years I've had the privilege of meeting regularly with a group of godly men to pray for one another—but mostly to pray for others. We've usually met early in the morning before heading off to work.

This hour together once a week has come to be one of the most meaningful experiences in my Christian life. Together we've seen God answer prayers in our lives and in the lives of others. We've all experienced the encouragement that comes from mutually sharing *and* bearing one another's burdens.

This book has grown out of personal experience, both in being a part of a group of praying Christians and through sharing these principles with the body of believers I serve as senior pastor. Hopefully, all of us who worship together at Fellowship Bible Church are praying more and experiencing more of God's life and work within us and through us because of the truths in this book.

My prayer is that your perspective on prayer will be expanded as you read this book. Most of all, I'm hopeful your prayer life with others will be deepened and enriched.

"Therefore . . . pray for each other" (James 5:16).

GENE A. GETZ

Acknowledgment

First, I want to thank the men I pray with weekly. Each Thursday at 6 A. M., a group of us who pastor and shepherd people at Fellowship Bible Church North meet to pray for these people and for one another. All of these men, both church staff and businessmen, have helped make the concepts in this book a reality in my life.

Second, I want to express my appreciation to the body at large at Fellowship Bible Church North for their positive reactions to the concepts in this book. As with most manuscripts I've authored in recent years, I first shared this material with them. Their responsiveness to my messages was personally encouraging and motivated me to prepare this material for use by the church at large.

Third, I want to thank Peter Hook and his wife, Carolyn, for their personal evaluation of this material. Peter serves as the primary pastor of Fellowship Bible Church in Duncanville, Texas. Carolyn has faithfully served as my administrative assistant, managing both my pastoral ministry at Fellowship Bible Church and my responsibilities as director of the Bible Center for Church Renewal. I'm deeply indebted to their own perceptive insights, both into Scripture and in working with people. Thanks, Peter and Carolyn, for your encouragement.

Why Another Book on Prayer?

This book on prayer is different from most. For one thing, it focuses on *corporate* or "body" praying. Most books written on prayer emphasize personal or individual praying. This of course is important, but the subject of corporate prayer has been neglected. This is surprising since the references to prayer in the Book of Acts are almost exclusively corporate.

This observation leads to a second reason the emphasis in this book is different from most. The theme developed in each chapter follows the chronological development and growth of the church in the Book of Acts. We will observe the New Testament church at prayer.

In this sense the book is *ecclesiological* in its emphasis. It traces the development of the prayer life of the church from the time Christ ascended to the first prayer meeting on the Day of Pentecost; from the church in Jerusalem to the church at Antioch; from the churches established on the missionary journeys to the letters Paul eventually wrote to these churches from a Roman prison.

This book is designed to help you as an individual develop a more effective prayer life and to help you "help others" do the same. Furthermore, it will help the people in your church discover the joy and excitement of "praying for one another," and experience answered prayer as never before.

Each chapter concludes with a challenge—a life response section, giving you practical ideas for applying the biblical principles outlined in this book. You will get the most from this book if you not only read it on your own, but also study it with a group. This will give you an opportunity to interact with the material at an intellectual and emotional level, and to mutually encourage one another to apply the concepts immediately. In this sense, the group you study with will serve as a laboratory for learning—and growing in Jesus Christ.

1

A Biblical Priority

Some Thoughts on Prayer

Somehow, the simple act of prayer links a sovereign
God to a finite man. When man prays, God responds.
Difficult situations change. Unexplained miracles occur
(Dick Eastman, *The Hour That Changes the World,*
Baker Book House, p. 13).

In prayer you align yourselves to the purpose and
power of God and He is able to do things through you
that He couldn't do otherwise. For this is an open
universe, where some things are left open, contingent
upon our doing them. If we do not do them, they will
never be done, for God has left certain things open
to prayer—things which will never be done except
as we pray (Helen Smith Shoemaker quoting E. Stan-
ley Jones, *The Secret of Effective Prayer,* Word Books,
p. 15).

Prayer is the slender nerve that moveth the muscles
of omnipotence (Charles Spurgeon, *Twelve Sermons
on Prayer,* Baker Book House, p. 31).

Prayer has obtained things that seemed impossible and out of reach. It has won victories over fire, air, earth, and water. Prayer opened the Red Sea. Prayer brought water from the rock and bread from heaven. Prayer made the sun stand still. Prayer brought fire from the sky on Elijah's sacrifice. Prayer overthrew the army of Sennacherib. Prayer has healed the sick. Prayer has raised the dead. Prayer has procured the conversion of countless souls (J.C. Ryle, *A Call to Prayer,* Baker Book House, pp. 14-15).

Indeed, God has said nothing lies beyond the potential of prayer. Beloved, let us ask with new confidence ... Lord, teach us to pray! (Dick Eastman, *The Hour That Changes the World,* p. 19)

Gaining Perspective

This book presents a series of lessons on prayer, which really is nothing new. Many sermons have been preached and lectures given on this subject. Probably more books have been written on prayer than on any other biblical subject.

Personal Prayer. Most of what has been preached, taught, and written about prayer has focused on personal and private prayer rather than corporate and relational prayer. Private prayer is certainly emphasized and illustrated in the Bible, particularly in the Old Testament and in the Gospels. But the most prominent illustrations in the Book of Acts and the New Testament epistles are centered on the church gathered to pray. There is a reason for this change and emphasis, which we will consider later.

Let me offer an explanation for the abundance of material regarding private prayer. First, the Bible has a lot to say about this kind of praying. It should be a very important part of every Christian's life. It is modeled by Old Testament greats—men like Daniel, who knelt and prayed in his home three times a day (Dan. 6:10). And Nehemiah's prolonged period of prayer and fasting over the distressful situation in Jerusalem gives us another unique example. (For a detailed study on Nehemiah's prayer life, see the author's book *Nehemiah: A Man of Prayer and Persistence* [Regal]. Note particularly chapter 1, "Nehemiah's Perspective on Prayer.")

We know more about David's prayer life than any other Old Testament character. He wrote numerous psalms, which in themselves are prayers. These prayers are rich in content and can be used word for word by 20th-century Christians.

In the New Testament, Jesus Christ Himself modeled personal and private prayer continually. The Apostle Paul also made numerous references to his private prayer life in his letters to the churches.

Western Culture. It is understandable why so much has been written and presented on personal prayer. But why have we neglected the *corporate* emphasis on prayer found in the Book of Acts and the Epistles? Since this biblical content relates specifically to the life of the church, the body of Christ, it's here we discover the most relevant biblical teaching on prayer for 20th-century Christians.

The answer, I believe, relates to our culture and how it has influenced biblical interpretation. The hallmark of Western civilization has been rugged individualism. Because of our philosophy of life, we are used to the personal pronouns *I* and *my* and *me*. We have not been taught to think in terms of *we* and *our* and *us.* Consequently we "individualize" many references to corporate experience in the New Testament, thus often emphasizing personal prayer, personal Bible study, personal evangelism, and personal Christian maturity and growth. The facts are that more is said in the Book of Acts and the Epistles about corporate prayer, corporate learning of biblical truth, corporate evangelism, and corporate Christian maturity and growth than about the personal aspects of these Christian disciplines.

Don't misunderstand. Both are intricately related. But the personal dimensions of Christianity are difficult to maintain and practice consistently unless they grow out of a proper corporate experience on a regular basis. Therefore, this book begins where the history of the church begins—in the Book of Acts—and then moves chronologically and sequentially from that point. The emphasis in the scriptural record is clearly on *corporate prayer* being the context in which *personal prayer* becomes meaningful.

The Church. When the church was introduced to the world, it was a new phenomenon. There had been nothing like it ever before in history. With it came a whole new dynamic, new relationships, unique functions and purposes. It was God's special creation for a particular moment in history. Jesus Christ laid the groundwork for this special assembly of believers, and the Book of Acts records the history of the early church. The Epistles were later written to the locally established churches.

An Upper Room Experience

Following Christ's ascension, the first activity His followers engaged in was corporate prayer. They had just returned from the Mount of Olives where Jesus spoke His departing words (Acts 1:7-8). He then "was taken up before their eyes, and a cloud hid Him from their sight" (v. 9). While they looked "intently up into the sky as He was going," there appeared "two men dressed in white" who informed them that Jesus would someday return just as He had promised (vv. 10-11).

Luke then informs us that the disciples returned to Jerusalem and went immediately to an upstairs room where they had been staying. Present were the 11 apostles plus other close friends and relatives of Jesus. We read, "They all joined together constantly in prayer" (v. 14).

Strictly speaking, the church had not yet come into existence. Most Bible expositors believe the church was officially launched on the Day of Pentecost, the final day of the 50-day celebration for all God-fearing Jews. But practically speaking, those who formed the nucleus of the church in Jerusalem were already practicing one of its most important functions—corporate prayer.

For most of these followers of Jesus, this was a new experience, even for the Apostles. In fact, any kind of consistent prayer was a new experience for these Jewish Christians. Though they had often observed Jesus going into a private place to pray to His heavenly Father, we have no record that these first believers ever spent regular time in prayer, either together or alone.

We do know that the apostles observed the Lord praying. Following this experience, they asked Him to teach them to pray—which, of course, the Lord did (Luke 11:1-2). But even then they had a difficult time handling the discipline of prayer. This was dramatically illustrated when Jesus was praying alone in the garden prior to His death. During this agonizing experience for our Lord, the apostles all fell asleep. Understandably, they were "exhausted from sorrows" (Luke 22:45). This incident shows us their humanness. But it also points up the fact that prayer was not a significant priority in their lives. They would not watch and pray with Christ even for one hour (Mark 14:37).

The 20th-Century Church

As Christians, we cannot ignore the fact that the first activity these New Testament Christians engaged in was corporate prayer. Together they communed with God. We will see in future chapters what was begun as a priority continued as a priority.

When we first founded Fellowship Bible Church in Dallas and formed our leadership team of elders, we made prayer a definite priority. When we met to discuss the church's needs, we would pray and seek God's will before we made decisions. Once we made decisions, we would often pause and ask God to help us implement those decisions appropriately.

We also set up regular weekly sessions when we met as spiritual leaders to pray for specific needs among the congregation. Eventually we were praying for hundreds of people by name. Though we'd rise early in the morning to attend these prayer sessions, they were some of the most meaningful times of fellowship in our ministry as a leadership team.

This was a new experience for me. In my previous dealings with other churches, leadership meetings were business sessions—not decision-making prayer sessions. We did not meet to pray for people, but to transact business.

If spiritual leaders don't meet regularly to pray, eventually prayer will be de-emphasized in the body at large, both in teaching on the subject as well as in actual practice. This is easy to understand, for it is difficult to preach and teach something that is personally neglected.

On the other hand, when spiritual leaders emphasize prayer for people, an unusual unity develops in the leadership team and consequently in the church body. Both church leaders and individual members grow spiritually. Leaders not only stay in touch with members, but they also know their needs and concerns. As a result, leaders make decisions more in line with members' needs.

When prayer ceases to be a priority among spiritual leaders, problems gradually arise. Leaders lose contact with church members and become more "program" oriented than "people" oriented. They spend lots of time in business meetings trying to make decisions, often on their own. In some instances, church leaders end up making serious mistakes. Most of all, they lose touch with one another as leaders.

When this happens, church leaders become more concerned about themselves than other Christians. Eventually they move away from being servants to the body. And all of this affects the body at large—their own attitudes and their own prayer practices.

Whenever we as Christians de-emphasize prayer, we make ourselves vulnerable to Satan's evil darts. When this important piece of God's armor is missing, Satan will attack us at our point of weakness.

An Exhortation

After instructing the Ephesian Christians to put on the "full armor of God," Paul outlined what this "full armor" was. He wrote:

- Stand firm with the belt of truth buckled around your waist.
- Stand firm with the breastplate of righteousness in place.

- Stand firm with your feet fitted with the readiness that comes from the Gospel of peace.
- Take up the shield of faith.
- Take the helmet of salvation and the sword of the Spirit, which is the Word of God (Eph. 6:14-17).

Paul then concluded with this exhortation to prayer: "Pray in the Spirit on all occasions with all kinds of prayers and requests. With this in mind, be alert, and always keep on praying for all the saints" (v. 18).

To pray for all the saints means to pray for one another. We must never neglect this important exercise. If we do, Satan will attack us individually and collectively.

In these verses, Paul was discussing a corporate exercise. His instructions were specifically directed to the Ephesian church. The body in general was to put on the armor of God. This is obvious from the overall context of the Ephesian letter, the plural pronouns Paul used, and the analogy itself. Certainly it applies to *every* Christian individually, but its primary meaning related to the total body of believers at Ephesus.

A Personal Priority

Many factors can cause problems in a church. On the basis of Paul's warning as well as from personal experience, I am convinced that one primary factor is lack of corporate prayer. As a pastor I have determined by God's grace to always make prayer a priority—both in the church where I serve and in my own life.

Part of Satan's strategy is to get us so busy with other things—even good things—that we fail to give prayer its proper place. It's a natural tendency, especially when things are going well. But Scripture shows that prayer ranks high on God's priority list. And when prayer is neglected or missing, Satan will attempt to hurt the church, particularly through destroying unity.

Thank God we know what Satan's strategy is and how to defeat him. We have no excuse for allowing Satan to defeat us. When he does, we bear the responsibility. We must put on the "whole armor of God"—and make corporate prayer a priority.

A Challenge

How important is corporate prayer in your church? The following questions will help you determine to what extent it is a
priority in your church.

1. What planned opportunities are there for people in your
church to *pray for one another?* List those opportunities:

_____

_____

_____

_____

2. To what extent are people open and honest about their
needs? Instead are they fearful and reticent in sharing their
concerns? If so, why is this true?

3. Is prayer a natural and spontaneous part of your corporate life together, or is it overly "programmed"?

NOTE: There must be planned opportunity for prayer or it
will not take place. However, certain kinds of programmed
prayer can become mechanical, laborious, and unrelated to
reality.

4. To what extent is prayer—both corporate and personal—a priority in your own life?

NOTE: The extent to which you feel free to initiate spontaneous prayer with others in the church may indicate whether your
church leaders are modeling this process. Be careful, however,
not to judge others at this point. Rather, use the following
prayer to evaluate yourself. Ask God to change your life and
the lives of others in the church.

Lord, help me to make prayer a priority in my life,
not only personally, but also corporately in my church.
In my private prayers, help me to pray daily for the
leaders of my church. Help me also to be alert to the
prayer needs of others in the body.

A Project
Invite a small group of Christian friends to join you in studying this book. For most effective results, meet together once a week for 13 successive weeks.

A Unique Privilege

While speaking at a family conference in Forest Home, California, my wife and I met a missionary who had been teaching in Red China after the borders were open for more communication with the free world. She told us of a pastor and his little congregation who had been in prison for nearly 20 years. With the coming of greater religious freedom, they were all released from prison. This missionary told how she had observed this pastor and his flock, participating in their first communion and prayer service in a farm barnyard. Tears flowed from their faces as they lifted their voices in praise to God. It was a sight to behold—one never to be forgotten by the missionary who had never experienced religious persecution and imprisonment.

It is so easy for us to take our privileges for granted. In fact, sometimes we don't even know how privileged we are until we face a crisis. Then suddenly we have a much deeper appreciation of what we have.

As Christians, we often take prayer for granted. In this chapter we will see why prayer is such a unique privilege and learn to understand more fully our rights and privileges as believers.

Prayer was the disciples' first corporate activity following Christ's return to heaven. Luke records, "They all joined together constantly in prayer, along with the women and Mary the mother of Jesus, and His brothers" (Acts 1:14). Prayer was a *priority*.

But for them it was also a privilege. Because of their religious background, they would be unusually appreciative of this opportunity for *all* of them—leaders and laymen, men and women—to fellowship with God in a personal way. Why was this true?

A New and Living Way

Jesus Christ introduced a startling new concept to worship generally and prayer particularly. The author of the letter to the Hebrews explains this concept in detail in chapters 4–10. He then summarizes it succinctly:

> Therefore, brothers, since we have confidence to enter the most holy place by the blood of Jesus, by a new and living way opened for us through the curtain, that is, His body, and since we have a Great Priest over the house of God, let us draw near to God with a sincere heart in full assurance of faith" (Heb. 10:19-22).

The First Convenant (Heb. 9:1-7). For some 20th-century Christians, these verses (Heb. 10:19-22) may sound strange. Words and phrases like *most holy place, curtain,* and *Great Priest* can only be understood clearly by reviewing Old Testament passages where God instructed Moses to build the tabernacle. The writer of the Book of Hebrews reviews this for us in Hebrews 9:1-7.

THE TABERNACLE. This Old Testament place of worship was built at Mount Sinai after God delivered the Children of Israel from Egyptian bondage. The tabernacle proper was composed of two main compartments—the holy place and the most holy place. The tabernacle was also surrounded by a fence forming what was called the outer court. (See Figure 1.)

In the outer court stood the brazen altar where animals were sacrificed to God. The laver stood about midway between the altar and the tabernacle itself and served as a basin the priests used for ceremonial washings.

In the first part of the tabernacle—called the holy place—

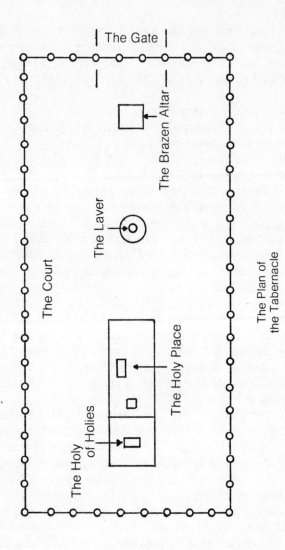

Figure 1

stood the table of showbread, the golden candlesticks, and the altar of incense.

The second compartment was called the most holy place or the holy of holies. It was separated from the holy place by a veil or a screen. Inside the most holy place rested the ark of the covenant—a chest measuring 3 3/4' long x 2 1/2' wide x 2 1/4' high. It was made of acacia wood and was overlaid with pure gold. The ark contained the two tablets of stone on which God had written the Ten Commandments. There was also a container of manna—reminding the Israelites how God had supernaturally provided for their physical needs. The third item was Aaron's rod that had budded. On top of the ark was the mercy seat—a lid of solid gold.

On both ends of the lid covering the ark stood two cherubs. They no doubt looked like human beings except for their wings. These symbolic figures stood facing each other as they looked down on the mercy seat. It was here in the holy of holies above the mercy seat and between the cherubim that God's presence dwelt in a very special way. He appeared in a cloud which was called the Shekinah.

Because Jehovah God revealed His presence in the holy of holies, ordinary people could not enter. Only the appointed high priest could enter this place, but only once a year. If the high priest ever entered the holy of holies without proper ceremonial preparation involving a blood sacrifice, he would die. Such was the awesomeness of God's holy presence.

THE TEMPLE. Later, the tabernacle, which was God's special dwelling place in Israel for 400 years, was replaced by Solomon's temple. The temple was destroyed by the Babylonians shortly after Solomon died. But under Zerubbabel's leadership, it was rebuilt when the Jews returned from captivity. This temple stood for approximately 500 years.

The most elaborate temple was built by Herod. This structure was still standing when Christ walked the earth, but it was destroyed by the Romans in A.D. 70.

Though each temple was a larger and more complex structure, each contained a section very similar to the tabernacle, which included both the holy place and the most holy place. During the time that these temples stood, God-fearing Jews practiced the same form of worship instituted in the wilderness at Mount Sinai. God-fearing Jews are still looking forward to the fulfillment of God's promise that the temple will be rebuilt (Ezek. 40—46).

The New Covenant (Heb. 9:11-15). When Jesus Christ came into this world He established a New Covenant based on His death and resurrection.

He became the perfect sacrifice for sin. When He died, the veil in the temple was supernaturally torn from the top to the bottom, indicating that nothing stands between God and anyone who has placed his faith in Jesus Christ for forgiveness of sins. Each of us can enter into the most holy place—God's very presence—anytime and anywhere.

We no longer need an intercessor or priest. Jesus Christ Himself is our great High Priest. The cross replaced the brazen altar. Christ's ability to cleanse us from all sin replaced the laver. As the Light of the world and the Bread of life, Christ replaced the golden candlestick and the table of showbread. As our constant Intercessor, He replaced the altar of incense. With His rent body which was torn by the nails and spear, He removed the veil which separated sinful mankind from God's holy presence. The sacrifice of Himself was "once for all" (Heb. 7:27). And once He offered Himself, He then "sat down on the right hand of the throne of the majesty in heaven" to intercede for His children (8:1).

Before Christ died and ascended to heaven, His disciples knew nothing of the great privilege they would soon experience. No ordinary Jew would consider entering into either the holy place or the most holy place in the temple. Only those who were priests could periodically enter the holy place, and only the high priest could enter the holy of holies. Spontaneous and personal communion with God in prayer was not a natural and normal experience for most of the people in Israel. That's one reason why the apostles were so interested in Christ's prayer life and why they asked Him to teach them to pray.

A New Testament Illustration (Luke 1:5-10). Luke gives us some helpful information about the worship experiences of Jews at the time Christ appeared on earth. Zechariah, the father of John the Baptist, is identified as a priest who lived during the reign of King Herod (Luke 1:5). History tells us he was 1 priest among nearly 18,000.

These priests were divided into 24 divisions, and Zechariah "belonged to the priestly division of Abijah" (v. 5). Though sacrifices were offered in the temple twice each day—morning and evening—only selected priests from each of these 24 divisions performed these duties.

On one occasion Zechariah "was chosen by lot . . . to go into the temple of the Lord and burn incense" (Luke 1:9). This was a great privilege! Since priests were so numerous, they cast lots to see who would participate in this significant worship function. How great this privilege was becomes obvious when we understand that the opportunity to burn incense—symbolic of prayer— came to a priest only *once* in his lifetime—if he was fortunate enough to be chosen. Some priests never were.

Luke gives us another helpful insight in verse 10. He wrote, "And when the time for the burning of incense came, all the assembled worshipers were praying outside."

Notice the words *time, outside,* and *praying* in this verse. First, the Jews were "schedule" oriented in their religious life. Worship and prayer were regimented and determined by the activities of the priests. Thus, the people waited till the proper time or hour.

Second, people in general could never enter the holy place, let alone the holy of holies. This was why they remained outside.

Third, their prayers were limited in scope and related to the specific actions of their priests and earthly representatives before God. In his commentary on Luke, Howard Marshall points out that the Jews' prayer as they stood outside was a simple request—"May the merciful God enter the holy place and accept with favor the offering of His people" (*Commentary on Luke,* William B. Eerdmans, p. 54). They had no firm assurance God would respond to them, accept their offering, and forgive their sins.

Let Us Draw Near

When Jesus Christ died, arose again, and ascended into heaven, He changed the way we worship. Now we can enter the most holy place with confidence (Heb. 4:16). We can boldly approach God because Christ's blood was shed once for all the sins of the world. Christ is our Great Priest.

Consequently, Christians are told to "draw near to God with a sincere heart in full assurance of faith" (10:22). We can be confident He will hear us and not reject us. We should no longer have guilty consciences. We have been "washed with pure water" (v. 22); that is, we've been cleansed once for all by the blood of Jesus Christ.

After Christ ascended to heaven, the disciples began immediately to avail themselves of the great privilege of prayer. Though they still had much to learn about their privileges as Christians, they understood in part at least that the Old Covenant had been superceded by the New. Prayer became the natural means by which they communicated their thoughts and feelings to God. Jesus Christ was their Great Priest, interceding for them and representing them before the Father.

Every Christian since that time has had the same privilege. We no longer need human priests to represent us before God. Paul later made this point when he wrote, "There is one God and one Mediator between God and man, the man Christ Jesus, who gave Himself as a ransom for all men" (1 Tim. 2:5-6).

A Word to 20th-Century Christians

Prayer, then, is a great privilege! In fact, it is one of the greatest privileges we have. It is far greater than being born in a free society; than being born into a wealthy family—even a Christian family.

To enter God's presence is the greatest privilege known to man. We no longer have to "come to a mountain . . . that is burning with fire; to darkness, gloom, and storm; to a trumpet blast or to such a voice speaking words, so that those who heard it begged that no further word be spoken to them" (Heb. 12:18-

20). In those days, if even an animal touched the mountain, it had to be stoned. "The sight was so terrifying that Moses said, 'I am trembling with fear' " (v. 21).

Rather, we "have come to Mount Zion, to the heavenly Jerusalem, the city of the living God." We "have come to thousands upon thousands of angels in joyful assembly, to the church of the firstborn, whose names are written in heaven." We "have come to God, the Judge of all men, to the spirits of righteous men made perfect, to Jesus the Mediator of a New Covenant, and to the sprinkled blood that speaks a better world than the blood of Abel" (vv. 22-24).

This privilege becomes even more significant when we realize that it cost the greatest price ever paid—the death of the Son of God on Calvary's cross. As Elvina M. Hall wrote:

> Jesus paid it all,
> All to Him I owe;
> Sin had left a crimson stain,
> He washed it white as snow.

Unfortunately many of us take our privileges for granted. What will it take for us to really appreciate all that we have, not only in and through our Lord Jesus Christ, but in our free society?

A Challenge

What about prayer? Do we comprehend how privileged we are? If we really did, wouldn't we be more diligent in prayer? Wouldn't our hearts be more warm and responsive to God?

As 20th-century Christians we are 2,000 years removed from Christ's death, resurrection, and ascension. We're 2,000 years removed from Pentecost and the coming of the Holy Spirit. Unfortunately we are 2,000 years from that firsthand experience of being able to enter for the first time into the Lord's presence freely, at any time and any place.

But thank God we have the Bible, God's divinely inspired record of these events. Hopefully this book will help us:

- To *know* how great our privilege of entering God's presence through prayer really is.
- To deeply *appreciate* this privilege.
- To *practice* this privilege more diligently, both in personal and corporate prayer.

Check yourself with these questions:

	A Little	**Some**	**Much**
1. How much do I really *understand* this privilege?	☐	☐	☐
2. How much do I really *appreciate* this privilege?	☐	☐	☐
3. How often do I *practice* this privilege?	☐	☐	☐

NOTE: A lot of Christians, if perfectly honest, would have to check "much" for *understanding;* "some" for *appreciation;* and "a little" for *practice*. What about you?

A Final Thought

True Christianity involves three dimensions—knowing, feeling, and doing! Pray:

Father, thank You for the privilege of entering Your holy presence through prayer—at any time and in any place. Thank You that I can approach Your "throne of grace with confidence" in order that I may receive mercy and find grace to help in my time of need. Thank You for Jesus Christ who sits at Your right hand representing me and serving as my Mediator. May I never take this privilege for granted.

A Project

Ask your closest Christian friend to read this chapter. Then discuss it together, setting up some personal and corporate goals.

3

A Steadfast Process

Most of us have been impressed with the stories of great men and women of God—people the Lord used in special ways to accomplish His work. One of their primary secrets, we're told, involved the *time* they devoted to prayer. For example, Samuel Rutherford, renowned Scottish pastor and theologian who accomplished many things for Christ, rose each morning at 3 to converse with God. John Welch, a man God used dramatically to touch thousands of lives with revival, once remarked "that his day was ill spent if he could not stay 8 or 10 hours in secret solitude" (Dick Eastman, *No Easy Road,* Baker Book House, p. 13).

It is also reported that Bishop Andrews, a great missionary to India, spent more than 5 hours daily in prayer and Bible study. And Charles Simeon used to rise each day and kneel to pray from 4 to 8. Martin Luther once stated: "If I fail to spend 2 hours in prayer each morning, the devil gets the victory for the day" (Eastman, *No Easy Road,* p. 14).

As a young Christian, I was both impressed and discouraged with the stories of these devout people. I was impressed because I admired their commitment to Jesus Christ and their willingness to devote so much time to prayer. But I was discouraged because their prayer life made mine seem as nothing. I wondered if God could ever use me.

I'm sure my experience is not unusual. What *is* God's plan for Christians? How much time *does* He expect us to spend in prayer? To answer these questions, we need to look again at both the prayer life of New Testament Christians and the specific instructions that were given to them.

From Acts 1:14 we've already observed that prayer was a *priority* for these New Testament Christians. Making prayer a priority was definitely related to the fact that prayer was a new and unique privilege. With Christ's death, resurrection, and ascension, God opened up direct access to His throne through the once-for-all and perfect sacrifice of Jesus Christ.

But we can learn more about the prayer life of these believers from Acts 1:14. Prayer was also a *process.* The dictionary defines *process* as a "continuous action." It certainly describes the prayer life of these Jerusalem Christians. We read that they "all joined together *constantly* in prayer."[1] This verse in the *New American Standard Bible* reads that these Christians 'were *continually devoting* themselves to prayer." The idea in the *Greek New Testament* literally means to "continue steadfastly" in prayer.

What relevance does this biblical observation about prayer have for our lives? What can and should we learn?

What It Doesn't Mean

To discover what this biblical example actually means for us, let's look first at what it doesn't mean.

The Scriptures do not teach that prayer is the only function that Christians should engage in on a continuous basis. Prayer was only one of several regular experiences that the Jerusalem Christians practiced as a corporate body. As Luke recorded the history of the church, he made this clear. After the Holy Spirit came on the Day of Pentecost, actually giving birth to the church, the small group of believers that initially met to pray in the Upper Room grew rapidly. Many Jews responded to the Apostle Peter's message on repentance (Acts 2:14-40). We

---

[1]Hereafter, all italicized words in Scripture references are for author's emphasis.

read that "those who accepted his message were baptized, and about 3,000 were added to their number that day" (v. 41).

Luke then records that these new believers "devoted themselves to the apostles' teaching and to the fellowship, to the breaking of bread and to prayer" (v. 42). There are actually two continuous functions described in this verse.

Continuing in the Apostles' Teachings. First, they "devoted themselves to the apostles' teaching." In essence, the apostles were particularly gifted by the Holy Spirit to teach and communicate God's eternal truth. Jesus had told them that He would send them "another Counselor" (John 14:16). Jesus identified this Counselor as "the Spirit of Truth" (v. 17), who would "teach you all things" and "remind you of everything" (v. 26).

In Acts 2:42 Luke describes the beginning steps in the fulfillment of this promise. Indwelt and inspired by the Holy Spirit, the apostles were able to teach God's truth. In some miraculous way, God touched their memories and enabled them to recall and share the truth they had heard previously from the lips of Jesus. Not only did they recall it, but they then understood it.

Furthermore, the Holy Spirit enabled them to teach additional truths. Jesus had told them He had "much more to say" to them, but it was more than they could accept and understand. "But," Jesus continued, "when He, the Spirit of Truth, comes, He will guide you into all truth" (16:12-13).

Again Christ's promise was being fulfilled. That day in Jerusalem, the apostles spoke the Word of God guided by the Holy Spirit. In days to come, they would share even more, not only in oral form but in written form. Consequently, we have available today our New Testament. In fact, the New Testament is primarily made up of documents written by the apostles, particularly Peter, John, and the man who later became the great missionary to the Gentiles—the Apostle Paul. In essence, the New Testament *is* "the apostles' teaching."

These new believers then "devoted themselves to the apostles' teaching." The word used here by Luke in the *Greek New Testament* to describe this learning process is identical to that used in Acts 1:14 to describe their prayer process. In fact, the

King James Version reads, "they continued steadfastly in the apostles' doctrine."

Continuing in Fellowship. The second continuous function engaged in by the Jerusalem Christians was *fellowship,* which in turn included two other specific experiences. Thus we read, "They devoted themselves . . . to the fellowship, to the breaking of bread, and to prayer" (v. 42). Here Luke is describing two interrelated functions: communion and prayer.

The first involves remembering the Lord's broken body and shed blood by means of a communion meal. In the same Upper Room where Jesus had promised to send the apostles "another Counselor," He introduced them to a new and deeper meaning in the Passover meal. As He took the bread (which was part of that meal), broke it, and shared it with the apostles, He said, "This is My body given for you; do this in remembrance of Me" (Luke 22:19). Then after the supper, He shared a special cup of wine with them saying, "This cup is the New Covenant in My blood, which is poured out for you" (v. 20).

When Jesus ascended into heaven, this was one of the profound truths that the Holy Spirit brought to the minds of the apostles. Though earlier they had not understood what Jesus meant, they now understood clearly, and taught these new Christians to do what Jesus had instructed.

In the early days of Christianity, the rather complex Passover meal which was practiced annually by faithful Jews became a common and regular experience among Christians. The elaborate and special meal was replaced by ordinary daily meals. In the context of a semi-communal society in Jerusalem, they used the common elements of their meals to remember the broken body and shed blood of Christ. This was one reason why it became a regular experience in fellowship and sharing.

The second aspect of this fellowship function was *prayer,* and as we've already noted, it became an intricate part of this communion meal. Thus we read, "They devoted themselves . . . to the breaking of bread and to prayer" (Acts 2:42).

Today, the full communion meal has been replaced in most churches with a token meal. This is understandable because private meetings were eventually outlawed in the Roman Empire, forcing Christians to hold meetings in public places. Consequently, the private, intimate home settings where they could "eat together" and "remember the Lord" were replaced with a much more simplified meal. However, this in no way should take away from the true meaning of communion, nor should it cause us to overlook the importance of including corporate prayer as a regular part of this overall fellowship experience.

We see then that prayer is not the only function that Christians should engage in on a *continuous* basis. We need regular opportunities:

- To learn God's Word.
- To remember the broken body and shed blood of Christ.
- To pray together.

As these functions are intertwined and interrelated, all of them become more meaningful and helpful. Prayer becomes a means by which we communicate our deepest thoughts and feelings to God. Furthermore, it is this overall context that keeps prayer vital, dynamic, and truly meaningful.

The Scriptures do not teach that continuous prayer involves mere repetition. Down through the years, Christians have practiced various forms of prayer. As a child, I remember kneeling by my bedside every night and saying:

Now I lay me down to sleep
I pray the Lord my soul to keep.
If I should die before I wake
I pray the Lord my soul to take.

In fact, at times when I got sleepy I found myself saying "Mary had a little lamb."

Certainly, there is nothing wrong in repeating well-worded prayers. In fact, Jesus Himself gave us a beautiful prayer that has been repeated again and again by devout Christians throughout the centuries. But when He shared this prayer with the disciples, He also warned them: "And when you pray, do not keep on babbling like pagans, for they think they will be heard because of their many words. Do not be like them, for your Father knows what you need before you ask Him" (Matt. 6:7-8).

What did Jesus mean? His main concern seemed to be on meaningless or "vain" repetitions—as translated in the *King James Version.* Non-Christian religions frequently promote prayer practices that encourage people to pray long and hard, believing that "the longer and louder they pray, the greater also will be their chance of success in receiving their desire" (William Hendricksen, *The Gospel of Matthew,* Baker Book House, pp. 324-325).

The prophets of Baal on Mount Carmel are a classic example of this kind of praying. Elijah had challenged them to a spiritual dual to demonstrate who was the one true God. The real test would be fire sent from heaven in answer to prayer.

The prophets of Baal agreed. All day "they called on the name of Baal." They "shouted" and "danced around the altar they had made." Elijah encouraged them to "shout louder"— which they did, but to no avail (1 Kings 18:26-29).

Elijah then called on God. His prayer was simple and direct:

O Lord, God of Abraham, Isaac, and Israel, let it be known today that You are God in Israel and that I am Your servant and have done all these things at Your command. Answer me, O Lord, answer me, so these people will know that You, O Lord, are God, and that You are turning their hearts back again (vv. 36-37).

God answered Elijah's prayer. Fire fell from heaven! The vain and continuous repetitions offered by the prophets of Baal failed. The primary reason, of course, is that they were praying to "gods" that in reality did not exist.

A more contemporary example involves the prayers of those who are involved in the Hare Krishna sect. Though they are not as public in their worship as they were several years ago, they frequently engage in repetitious chanting, believing that there is spiritual value in this religious exercise.

Still another example relates to the Tibetan Buddhists. They have inscribed prayers on a prayer wheel. As this cylinder revolves on an axis, they believe that there is efficacious value in turning this wheel. In other words, the continuous turning of the wheel transmits prayers to their deities.

When we consider these vain repetitions, we can understand more clearly what Jesus meant when He said to His followers— "Do not keep on babbling like pagans, for they think they will be heard because of their many words" (Matt. 6:7). The true and living God is not interested in "words" per se. Rather, He is more interested in our sincere desires, our motives, and our heart attitudes.

William Hendriksen points out that "many of the most striking and fervent prayers recorded in the Scriptures are brief" (*The Gospel of Matthew,* p. 324). He illustrates this with the prayers of Moses (Ex. 32:31-32), Solomon (1 Kings 3:6-9), Hezekiah (2 Kings 19:14-19), Jabez (1 Chron. 4:10), Agur (Prov. 30:7-9), the publican (Luke 18:13), the dying thief (Luke 23:42), Stephen (Acts 7:60), and Paul (Eph. 3:14-19). He also calls attention to Nehemiah's sentence prayers (Neh. 4:4-5; 5:19; 6:9; 13:14, 29, 31), Even Christ's prayers are relatively brief and to the point (John 17; Matt. 6:9-13; Luke 11:2-4).

What It Does Mean

What, then, does the example of the Jerusalem Christians mean to us?

Continuous prayer means consistent praying with other Christians. There is no question that God intended the Jerusalem Christians to be a model for believers of all times. Though the circumstances vary, affecting the degree and intensity of prayer, it is clear from the letters written to New Testament churches that what was happening in Jerusalem was to be an ongoing process. For example, in the practical sections in most of Paul's New Testament letters, he instructed Christians to make corporate prayer a regular and consistent part of their lives. Note the following directions:

- Be joyful in hope, patient in affliction, *faithful* in prayer (Rom. 12:12).
- And pray in the Spirit on *all occasions* with all kinds of prayers and requests (Eph. 6:18).
- Do not be anxious about anything but *in every-*

thing, by prayer and petition, with thanksgiving, present your requests to God (Phil. 4:6).
* *Devote yourselves* to prayer, be watchful and thankful (Col. 4:2).

In essence, all of these Scriptures are instructing Christians as a body of believers to be consistent in prayer. The context is clear that Paul first of all has in mind *corporate* praying. This does not mean he is excluding personal and private prayer, but he is emphasizing the importance of Christians meeting together—as the Jerusalem Christians—to pray.

Continuous prayer involves an attitude of prayer. For the Christian whose mind and heart are focused on God's Word and will, the very attitudes and thoughts of the heart *become* prayer. In this sense, we can indeed "pray without ceasing" (1 Thes. 5:17, KJV).

Relative to this concept, Theodore L. Cuyler comments, "Some people seem to regard prayer as a rehearsal of a set form of words, learned largely from the Bible or a liturgy; and when uttered they are only from the throat outward. Genuine prayer is a believing soul's direct converse with God. Phillip Brooks has condensed it into four words—a 'true wish sent Godward' " (*Daily Meditations for Prayer,* Good News Publishers, p. 41).

Nehemiah illustrated this kind of praying when King Artaxerxes asked him what he might do to help him solve the problem in Jerusalem. He had no opportunity to stop and spend time praying for an answer to the king's question. But we read, "Then I prayed to the God of heaven, and I answered the king" (Neh. 2:4-5). Nehemiah's prayer and answer were so interrelated they seem to be simultaneous events. In essence they were, for the very *desire* to respond appropriately became Nehemiah's prayer. God knew his heart.

Continuous prayer involves personal discipline. Few things in life are natural and easy to come by. And this is certainly true of prayer. Dick Eastman put it well in his book, *No Easy Road:*

To learn prayer men must pray. We learn prayer's deepest depths in prayer, not from books. We reach prayer's highest heights in prayer, not from sermons. The only place to learn prayer, is in prayer, bent and broken on our knees. Prayer is skill developed through experience. Learning to pray is like learning a trade. We are apprentices and must serve time at it. Consistent care, thought, practice, and time are needed to become a skillful prayer-er (p. 13).

A Challenge
The Bible does not specify how much time we should spend in prayer. The degree and intensity varies—depending on our needs, our responsibilities, and our calling in life. However, the Bible does make it very clear that *all* Christians should pray—consistently. It is to be a regular part of our daily lives—privately and together as Christians.

Evaluate the consistency of your own prayer life with these questions:
- In what ways can I be more *consistent* in prayer?
- What can I do to make an *attitude* of prayer a natural part of my total lifestyle?
- What specific things should I do to be more *disciplined* in prayer?

A Checklist
The following list of activities will help you improve the consistency of your prayer life:

1. Join a weekly prayer group.
2. Compile a prayer notebook.
3. Practice praying spontaneously about daily activities, asking for God's guidance.
4. Memorize Romans 12:12; Ephesians 6:18; Philippians 4:6; and Colossians 4:2.
5. Read some good books on prayer; for example, Dick Eastman's *The Hour That Changes the World* and *No Easy Road* (Baker Book House).
6. Discover someone who will be your special telephone prayer partner.

7. If a parent, lead your family in prayer before meals and at bedtime. Also, look for spontaneous moments to pray about special things.

8. Spend a day in prayer. Read *How to Spend a Day in Prayer* by Lorne C. Sanny (NavPress).

9. Other: _____

_____

> *Lord, help me to be faithful in prayer. Help me to "pray in the Spirit on all occasions with all kinds of prayers and requests." May I want to devote myself to prayer, to be watchful and always thankful.*

A Project

Select *one* activity from the checklist that is most related to your own needs. Write out a plan for implementing that activity. Then pray and ask God to help you follow through.

4
Godly Praise

When someone suggests spending some time in prayer, what's the first thing that goes through your mind? If you are like me, you think of human needs, concerns, problems—things to pray for—and about. Prayer sessions often begin with the question: What are your needs? We then spend time asking God for help. There are those who are ill, so we ask God to heal them. Someone's marriage is falling apart, so we ask God to help get it back together. Parents request prayer for their wayward children. Other Christians are facing financial stress. Still others need jobs. The list is endless, for everywhere Christians have needs and concerns.

In our Fellowship churches in Dallas, we structure a time in most of our regular services to give individual members opportunity to participate in an open sharing service. Over the years I've noticed that if the service is allowed to take its own course, people spend most of the time asking someone to pray for a special need—in their own life or in someone else's life.

Certainly, this is not wrong. Jesus Himself said, "Ask and it will be given to you; seek and you will find; knock and the door will be opened to you" (Matt. 7:7). And Paul urged Christians to pray "on all occasions with all kinds of prayer and requests" (Eph. 6:18). To the Philippians he wrote, "Do not be anxious about anything, but in everything, by prayer and petition, with thanksgiving, present your requests to God" (Phil. 4:6).

But prayer is more—much more—than asking. Prayer is also praising. In fact, that is where New Testament Christians began the prayer process.

An Observation

After these new believers returned to Jerusalem from the Mount of Olives where Jesus had ascended, they immediately began to pray. As we have seen, prayer indeed was a priority. But Luke also records for us the kind of prayer they engaged in initially. To gain this insight we need to turn to the last three verses of his Gospel record.

While He [Jesus] was blessing them, He left them and was taken up to heaven. Then they worshiped Him and returned to Jerusalem with great joy. And they stayed continually at the temple, *praising God* (Luke 24:51-53).

This passage from the Book of Luke gives us a clue about the kind of prayers these believers engaged in when they met in the Upper Room (Acts 1:14). It seems appropriate to conclude that the basic content of their prayers was an extension of the kind of prayers they were offering in the temple. These Christians probably spent time in the temple designated as the "hour of prayer" and when the time periods were over, they no doubt continued the process of prayer in another place—in this instance in the Upper Room.

The conclusion that the main ingredient in their prayers was initially *praise* is further reinforced in Acts 2:42-47. As we have seen, these Christians "devoted themselves to the apostles' teaching and to the fellowship, the breaking of bread and to prayer. Everyone was filled with awe, and many wonders and miraculous signs were done by the apostles" (vv. 42-43). Later we read, "They broke bread in their homes and ate together with glad and sincere hearts, *praising God*" (vv. 46-47). Here Luke seems to be giving a more specific description of the kind of praying they engaged in initially. Their focus was definitely on praise.

A Question

Why is this biblical observation so important? Though the Lord certainly wants us to bring our petitions and requests to Him, He wants us to do so with thanksgiving. He desires our praise and adoration. He wants us to think first of Him—not ourselves. This is why, when He taught His disciples to pray, His first statement was, "Our Father in heaven, hallowed be Your name, Your kingdom come, Your will be done on earth as it is in heaven" (Matt. 6:9-10).

Before instructing His disciples to ask for "daily bread," He exhorted them to acknowledge God's holiness, His greatness, and His sovereign plan.

Why emphasize praise in prayer first rather than petitions and requests? Dick Eastman writes, "Only praise puts God in His rightful position at the very outset of our praying. In praising God we declare His sovereignty and recognize His nature and power" (*The Hour That Changes the World,* Baker Book House, p. 23).

Harold Lindsell, speaking of the same concept, has written, "Since adoration brings man into immediate and direct contact with God, the role of servant to Master, or the created to the Creator, it is foundational to all other kinds of prayer" (*When You Pray,* Baker Book House, pp. 30-33).

Praise focuses on God's nature rather than on human needs. Paul Billheimer emphasizes this point. "Here is one of the greatest values of praise: it decentralizes self. The worship and praise of God demands a shift of center from self to God. One cannot praise God without relinquishing occupation with self. Praise produces forgetfulness of self—and forgetfulness of self is health" (*Destined for the Throne,* Christian Literature Crusade, p. 118).

A Dramatic Example

One outstanding example of focusing first on God rather than on personal needs is found in Acts 16. Paul and Silas had gone to the city of Philippi. There they encountered a slave girl who was demon possessed. Her owners used her as a fortune-teller—

to predict the future—and we're told that they were making "a great deal of money" (Acts 16:16).

One day while Paul and Silas were on their way to a prayer meeting, the girl followed them. She kept calling out, "These men are servants of the Most High God, who are telling you the way to be saved" (v. 17). Luke records further that "she kept this up for many days" (v. 18).

Paul had finally had enough. He turned and commanded the evil spirit to leave the girl. We read, "At that moment the spirit left her" (v. 18).

This was the beginning of trouble for Paul and Silas. The men who owned the slave girl were livid with anger. Their source of income was cut off. Consequently, they turned the city magistrates, as well as a large crowd of citizens against Paul and Silas. Eventually, the two were stripped and beaten and thrown into prison.

Bruised and bleeding, Paul and Silas found themselves in the "inner cell"—a place designed for hardened criminals and those who were to be executed. Their feet were placed in stocks, which obviously limited their movement and added to their terrible discomfort.

Paul and Silas' response to this experience is mind boggling. Around midnight they began to pray and sing hymns of praise to God (v. 25). There's no evidence that they asked God to deliver them from their dismal situation. There's no evidence they asked for healing. There's no evidence they even asked for strength to bear up under this ordeal. Rather, they *praised God in prayer!*

The response to their prayer and praise was dramatic. There was an earthquake! The prison foundations shook and all the doors flew open. Everyone's chains fell off.

The chief jailer, awakened, was panic-stricken. Seeing the doors open, he assumed everyone had escaped. Knowing he would be held responsible, he decided to take his own life before his superiors killed him.

In many respects, the end of the story is even more exciting and dramatic. Paul called to the jailer and stopped him from killing himself with his sword. Then Paul assured him the prisoners were all there. In response, the jailer ran to Paul and Silas and fell before them. Tremblingly, he asked how he too could be saved. Paul and Silas replied, "Believe in the Lord Jesus, and you will be saved" (v. 31). Hearing the Gospel clearly for the first time, the jailer and his whole household responded and later were baptized. No doubt his family became part of the initial nucleus of the church at Philippi.

20th-Century Lessons

There is a lesson in this story. It is *not* that we shouldn't *pray* when we are in trouble. There are many examples in Scripture where God's children cried out for assistance when facing difficulties. Furthermore, we are instructed to do so! What then is the lesson? *There are times we should praise God rather than ask for help or deliverance.*

This means focusing on God rather than on ourselves. In fact, God knows our hearts and, as in the situation faced by Paul and Silas, He may respond to our praise as readily as to our petitions.

Furthermore, some problems we face may be self-induced. The more we think about our problems—even in prayer—the worse they become.

There is no escape from self-pity quite so effective as to think about God and who He is! *When we gather together as Christians we must consistently include praise in our prayer and worship.*

In recent years we have experienced new emphasis on the functioning church. Some have called this the "body-life" movement. I have been involved in promoting as well as practicing this biblical concept, which I believe has been lost in many churches. In fact, this book is hopefully a further contribution to the "body-life" emphasis.

However, I am also concerned. I've seen Christians focus on human needs and problems and neglect worship and praise. I've seen Christians become inward and selfish in their prayer lives rather than focusing on God and others.

The answer is not either-or, but "both-and." The Christians in Jerusalem had dynamic fellowship with God *and* with one another.

Some of you know that I have helped start a number of churches in the Dallas metroplex. We've seen hundreds of people come to Christ, and we've seen many infant Christians begin to grow for the first time in their lives.

Many pastors, fellow missionaries, and other church leaders, having heard of what has transpired in Dallas, have come to visit our churches and to experience what God has done. Generally they have been rewarded, inspired, and impressed. But often they say something like this: "We really enjoy the Bible teaching and your emphasis on application and life response. We're impressed with Christians who are really concerned for one another and for reaching non-Christians. But what about worship and praise?"

I explain that we believe that the quality of our relationship with God is determined by the quality of our relationships with one another. I also emphasize that worship need not be planned to happen.

The facts are, however, the less we emphasize the "God-ward" dimension of Christian experience, the more we concentrate on ourselves—our needs, our concerns, and our problems. This is our natural direction. But there may be very little worship and praise *if* we don't plan for it.

This does not mean that we need to plan traditional worship services. Many of these services can quickly become mere routine, formal and meaningless. But we must plan for worship to happen on a consistent basis. We must encourage people to praise God.

Some Practical Suggestions

All that we say and do as Christians should be an act of spiritual worship and praise. Paul urged the Roman Christians to offer their bodies to Christ as an act of "spiritual worship." He said that they should not allow themselves to become conformed to this world's system (Rom. 12:1-2).

But in a special way, we as a body of believers should praise God with our lips. Thus we read, "Through Jesus, therefore, let us *continually* offer to God a sacrifice of praise—the fruit of lips that confess His name" (Heb. 13:15).

It is also quite clear from Scripture that one unique way Christians combined prayer and praise was with music—particularly by singing. This was true of Paul and Silas, even in a prison cell—and at midnight! When Paul later wrote to the Ephesians he instructed them to "speak to one another with psalms, hymns, and spiritual songs. Sing and make music in your hearts to the Lord," he continued, "always giving thanks to God the Father for everything, in the name of our Lord Jesus Christ" (Eph. 5:19-20).

This combination is also emphasized in the Psalms. In fact, many believe that when Paul and Silas were in prison, they were praising God in prayer by means of some of the Old Testament Psalms. Let's look at the Psalms and see what we can learn about prayer and praise.

How to Praise the Lord

Sing joyfully to the Lord, you righteous; it is fitting for the upright to praise Him. Praise the Lord with the harp; *make music* to Him on the 10-stringed lyre. *Sing to Him* a new song; *play skillfully,* and shout for joy (Ps. 33:1-3).

Sing praises to God, sing praises; sing praises to our King, sing praises. For God is the King of all the earth; *sing* to Him a psalm of praise (47:6-7).

Shout with joy to God, all the earth! *Sing* to the glory of His name; offer Him glory and praise! Say to God, "How awesome are Your deeds! So great is Your power that Your enemies cringe before You. All the earth bows down to You; they *sing praise* to You, they *sing praise* to Your name" (66:1-4).

I will praise You *with the harp* for Your faithfulness,
O my God; I will sing praise to You *with the lyre,* O
Holy One of Israel (71:22).

The Content of "Praise—Prayer"

Dick Eastman reminds us that "the possibilities for praise stretch
beyond the limits of our imagination. Because God has no limits,
our praise is limitless" (*The Hour That Changes the World,* p.
27).

This certainly is true. However, we must start somewhere,
and the Psalms again help us to know what to praise God for.
We should praise God for His *greatness.*

Clap your hands, all you nations; shout to God with
cries of joy. How *awesome* is the Lord Most High, the
great King over all the earth! (Ps. 47:1-2)

Praise be to the Lord God, the God of Israel, who
alone does *marvelous deeds* (72:18).

Great is the Lord and most worthy of praise; His
greatness no one can fathom (145:3).

We should praise God for His *love.*
Let them give thanks to the Lord for His unfailing
love and His wonderful deeds for men (107:8).

I have seen You in the sanctuary and beheld Your
power and Your glory. Because Your *love* is better
than life, my lips will glorify You (63:2-3).

We should praise God for His *protection.*
But I will sing of Your strength, in the morning I will
sing of Your love; for You are *my fortress, my refuge*
in times of trouble. O my Strength, I will sing praise
to You; You, O God, are my fortress, my loving God
(59:16-17).

We should praise God for *answered prayer.*
Praise be to God, who has not rejected my prayer or withheld His love from me! (66:20)

We should praise God for His *constant care.*
Praise be to the Lord, to God our Saviour, who *daily bears our burdens* (68:19).

We should praise God for His *faithfulness.*
I will praise You with the harp for Your *faithfulness,* O my God; I will sing praise to You with the lyre, O Holy One of Israel (71:22).

We should praise God for His *salvation.*
My lips will shout for joy when I sing praise to You— I, whom You have *redeemed* (71:23).

When to Praise God

I will extol the Lord at *all times;* His praise will *always* be on my lips. . . . But I will sing of Your strength, *in the morning* I will sing of Your love. . . . Praise be to His glorious name *forever;* may the whole earth be filled with His glory. Amen and Amen. . . . *Every day* I will praise You and extol Your name for ever and ever (Pss. 34:1; 59:16; 72:19; 145:2).

Where to Praise God

I will praise You *in the presence of Your saints.* . . . I will praise You, O Lord, *among the nations;* I will sing of You *among the peoples.* . . . Praise the Lord. Praise God *in His sanctuary;* Praise Him *in His mighty heavens* (Pss. 52:9; 57:9; 150:1).

A Challenge

• Using the Psalms outlined and quoted in this chapter, evaluate your *personal* prayer life. To what extent do you praise God?

• Also evaluate the prayer life of your *church*. To what extent do the Christians in your church really praise God? How can this aspect of your worship service be improved?

> *Father, Son, and Holy Spirit, I lift my voice to You in praise and with thanksgiving. I praise You for Your indescribable greatness, Your unfathomable love, Your persistent protection, Your answers to prayer, Your tender care, Your constant faithfulness, and Your eternal salvation.*
>
> *I want to praise You at all times—in the morning, at noon, and in the evening. I'll praise You among Your children, among the leaders of my church, among those who do not know You, and in the presence of Your whole creation. Praise be to Your glorious name forever. May the whole earth be filled with Your glory.*

A Project
Since this prayer is based on the biblical content of the Psalms, consider how you might use it on occasions as a part of your own public worship.

5

God's Power

No book ever written persistently compacts so much truth into one single statement as the Bible. This reality is certainly illustrated in Acts 1:14. From this verse and its context, we've already seen that the first thing the Christians did when returning from the Mount of Olives was to "all join together constantly *in prayer*." Prayer was a definite priority for them.

Secondly, we noted that prayer was a priority for these believers because of a unique and new *privilege*. No longer were they separated from God's holy presence by the veil in the temple. They began to exercise this privilege immediately.

Thirdly, Luke records that "they all gathered together *constantly* in prayer." For New Testament Christians, prayer was to become a steadfast *process*—an ongoing experience. This is affirmed frequently in the letters that were written to the churches. As we've seen, they were to be "faithful in prayer," to pray "on all occasions," and to pray about "everything."

Fourthly, we've noted that the initial context of this prayer was *praise*. Their focus was first and foremost on God—not on themselves.

There is yet a fifth truth about prayer in this single verse. We read that "they all *joined together* . . . in prayer." The *New American Standard Bible* makes it even clearer: "These all *with one mind* were constantly devoting themselves to prayer." This initial prayer experience was characterized by a great sense of oneness and unity.

A Broader Context

This was not an isolated experience for these Jerusalem Christians. It was ongoing, as illustrated in Acts 4:24, where Luke records that "they raised their voices *together* in prayer to God." Again, the *New American Standard Bible* captures the more literal meaning of this verse: "They lifted their voices to God with *one accord.*" The word in the *Greek New Testament* translated "with one accord" literally means "with one mind" and is the same word Luke used earlier in Acts 1:14.

The events leading up to this prayer in chapter 4 are in themselves significant. The church in Jerusalem had continued to grow and expand under the *divine* direction of the Holy Spirit and the *human* leadership of the apostles. Peter and John stand out because of their teaching and healing ministry. They had encountered a man outside the temple who had been crippled from birth. Through the power of Christ the man was healed, giving Peter and John an opportunity to bear witness to Jesus' death and resurrection before their fellow Jews.

The response to their message was dramatic. Thousands responded to Peter's message and believed in Christ (Acts 4:4). However, the Jewish leaders in Jerusalem were greatly disturbed with Peter and John and "put them in jail" (v. 3).

The next day they were brought before the Jewish leaders in the city and interrogated. These religious men were sincerely puzzled and they were attempting to discover *how* Peter and John were able to perform what was undeniably a miracle (v. 16).

Peter, serving as the spokesman, set the record straight. He reported that it was *not by their power* that this man had been healed, but rather by the *power of Christ.* Peter stated, "It is by the name of Jesus Christ of Nazareth, whom you crucified but whom God raised from the dead, that this man stands before you completely healed" (v. 10).

Though these words cut deeply into the hearts of these men, they could not deny what they were hearing and seeing. There stood a man with Peter and John who had been crippled for over 40 years. And everywhere "people were praising God for what had happened" (v. 21).

At this point the Jewish leaders were perplexed and mystified. They decided that all they could do was to warn these two apostles "*not* to speak or teach at all in the name of Jesus" (v. 18). After threatening them, they let them go.

Peter and John immediately "went back to their own people and reported all that the chief priests and elders had said to them" (v. 23). Then all the Christians who were gathered together "raised their voices *together* in prayer to God" (v. 24).

Luke records this prayer in detail (vv. 24-30). We're not sure who prayed it or of its form, but one thing is very clear. Everyone present was involved and unified in what was said.

A Larger Perspective

It is not coincidental that Luke records another historical statement immediately following this demonstration of unity in prayer. He wrote, "All the believers were *one in heart and mind*" (Acts 4:32). With this statement, Luke helps us to better understand the concept of Christian unity. To be able to "pray as one" indeed involves far more than agreeing to come together for the purpose of prayer. It involves our total life together. Unity in prayer presupposes all that we think and do.

Christ's Concern for Unity. Unity among His followers—then and now—was one of Christ's primary concerns before He was taken captive and crucified. He spoke about it often when He withdrew from the world at large and spent time with the apostles.

So much of what happened in the early days of the church relates back to certain basic truths Jesus taught the apostles in the Upper Room and immediately following as they left that sacred place and headed for the Garden of Gethsemane. He told them about the "Spirit of Truth" who would come and continue to teach them God's will so they could in turn teach a larger group of disciples. He also introduced them to the true meaning of the Communion meal and He gave them their greatest lesson in humility. If they were to eventually "pray in unity," they needed to learn the basis and larger context of unity.

Shortly before they entered the Upper Room, the disciples were arguing among themselves about who would be elected to sit on the Lord's right and left hand in the coming kingdom. They were anything but "one in heart and mind." They were each obsessed with selfish ambition.

In this context Christ taught them the secret to unity. They had to "love one another" as Christ loved them. Though the Lord was referring to a much deeper and sacrificial expression of love, He began by teaching them to wash one another's feet.

In their culture this was a simple and common expression of love. It would be similar to our taking a guest's coat when he entered our home or directing him to a lavatory so he could "wash up" for dinner.

It is true that well-to-do Jews had servants to do this menial task. But these followers of Jesus were far from well-to-do. The motives behind their actions were simply selfish. They were unwilling to serve one another even in the simplest way.

Christ's Prayer for Unity. It is understandable that Christ later prayed as He did for these men. He asked His Father that "all of them may be one"—that they might "be brought to complete unity" (John 17:21, 23). But more noteworthy than His prayer for these men is the fact that He broadened His prayer to include Christians of all time. In fact, what Christ prayed that day represents one of those occasions when He prayed specifically for 20th-century Christians. Thus John recorded these words of Jesus: "I pray also for *those who will believe in Me through their message*" (v. 20).

This prayer includes every individual who would thereafter come to Christ through the teaching ministry of the apostles. Since the apostles were the primary authors of Scripture, everyone who would believe because of the written Word of God would be included in this prayer, even after the apostles passed off the scene. That includes all of us today for it is through the

Scriptures that we have come to understand and believe in
Christ's message. It is also for this reason that we continue to
devote ourselves "to the apostles' teaching."

Paul's Concern and Prayer for Unity. What was begun and
illustrated in Acts 1:14 is also emphasized in Paul's letters to
the New Testament churches. Just as Christians were exhorted
to devote themselves to prayer on a *continual* basis, they were
also told to *maintain unity* among themselves. Furthermore,
maintaining this unity was frequently the focus of Paul's personal concern and prayers for various churches. Note the following
examples:

- Live in *harmony* with one another . . . . If it is possible, as far as it depends on you, live at *peace* with
  everyone . . . . May the God who gives endurance
  and encouragement *give you a spirit of unity* among
  yourselves as you follow Christ Jesus, so that with
  one heart and mouth you may glorify the God and
  Father of our Lord Jesus Christ . . . . I urge you,
  brothers, to watch out for those who cause *divisions*
  and put obstacles in your way that are contrary to
  the teaching you have learned (Rom. 12:16, 18;
  15:5-6; 16:17).

- I appeal to you, brothers, in the name of our Lord
  Jesus Christ, that *all of you agree* with one another
  so that there may be *no divisions* among you and
  that you may be *perfectly united in mind* and thought
  . . . . Finally, brothers, good-bye. Aim for perfec-
  tion, listen to my appeal, *be of one mind,* live in
  peace. And the God of love and peace will be with
  you (1 Cor. 1:10, 2 Cor. 13:11).

- Make every effort to keep the *unity of the Spirit*
  through the *bond of peace* . . . . It was He who gave
  some to be apostles, some to be prophets, some to
  be evangelists, and some to be pastors and teachers, to prepare God's people for works of service,

so that the body of Christ may be built up until we all reach *unity in the faith* and in the knowledge of the Son of God and become mature, attaining to the whole measure of the fullness of Christ (Eph. 4:3, 11-13).

- Whatever happens, conduct yourselves in a manner worthy of the Gospel of Christ. Then, whether I come and see you or only hear about you in my absence, I will know that you stand firm in *one spirit* contending as *one man* for the faith of the Gospel . . . . Then make my joy complete by being *like-minded,* having the same love, being *one in spirit and purpose* (Phil. 1:27; 2:2).

A Condition for Answered Prayer

It is clear from Scripture that Christian unity is to be the context in which prayer is to take place. But an even more significant relationship between unity and prayer is not only that it should exist, but that it is the context in which God's *power* is released. In fact, it is a basis for answered prayer.

Much could be said regarding the fact that love and unity among Christians is the means that God uses to release His power in various ways. However, let's limit our observations to the relationship between unity and answered prayer. (For a more in-depth treatment of how God releases His power through love and unity in the body of Christ, see the author's book, *Loving One Another,* also published by Victor. Note particularly chapters 8-9.)

Christ's Startling Statement. At one point in His teaching ministry, Jesus made a rather startling statement. Christ's disciples (probably the Twelve) had come to Him and were asking questions. The subject eventually turned to prayer and Jesus said, "Again, I tell you that if two of you on earth *agree* about anything you ask for, it will be done for you by My Father in heaven. For where two or three come together in My name, there am I with them" (Matt. 18:19-20).

Even though this statement is succinct, it is clear that Jesus had more in mind than merely "gathering together" to pray. The number of believers who gather is not the important point. Jesus is talking about *unity*—being *one* in heart and soul with others who gather. This is what is meant by the word *agree*.

However, the context makes Jesus' meaning even more clear. In verses 15-18, Jesus tells what a Christian should do when he is offended by another Christian. He unequivocally outlines the procedure that a Christian should follow—going first and speaking to that Christian alone. If there is no response, the one offended against confronts the other believer—this time with one or two others along. If there is still no response, the disagreement is to be taken to the larger assembly of believers.

If this procedure is violated in the church, there will be a very predictable result—disunity and eventually division. This has been verified again and again throughout church history. However, if we prayerfully follow this procedure, Satan will be defeated and unity will be maintained. Further, if we maintain unity, God responds to our prayers. It is implied that if we do not, God has not promised to respond.

The verses following Christ's "startling statement" also verify the relationship between unity and answered prayer. In the verses that precede His statement, Christ emphasized maintaining unity by following proper procedure when a Christian is offended. In the verses that follow the statement, He emphasized *forgiving* the offender.

Peter asked Jesus how many times he should forgive the brother who had sinned against him. When Peter asked if seven times was sufficient, Jesus responded with another startling statement: "I tell you, not seven times, but seventy-seven times" (Matt. 18:22).

There can be no unity among Christians without forgiveness. A believer who sins should be confronted through the proper procedure. If he does not respond, then he is not to be accepted as a part of the fellowship of the church. But when a brother sincerely asks forgiveness, he must be forgiven. Paul verifies this same emphasis when he later wrote, "Bear with each other and *forgive* whatever grievances you may have against one another. Forgive as the Lord forgave you" (Col. 3:13).

Bearing Fruit. Following Christ's teaching on confrontation and forgiveness and the relationship between unity and answered prayer, He dealt with the subject of unity again—and once again we pick up the continuity in the Upper Room discourse. Following Christ's lesson in humility with the foot-washing experience and following His promise that the Father would send the "Spirit of Truth," they left the Upper Room and descended into the streets of Jerusalem. As they walked, Jesus used a familiar setting to get across another point. No doubt passing a vineyard, He exhorted His followers to "bear fruit"—just as properly pruned branches bear fruit because of their relationship to the vine.

From the immediate context in John 15 as well as the larger context in chapters 13—17, Jesus shows that the "fruit" He is talking about is love (13:34-35; 15:9,12). If the disciples would bear this fruit, Jesus promised, "*Then* the Father will give you whatever you ask in My name" (15:16). To make sure His disciples knew what He was talking about, Jesus drove home the point once again, "This is My command: *Love each other*" (v. 17).

Christian love is the *basis* of unity. It reflects itself in oneness of heart, and when it is present, prayer becomes meaningful and effective. In this context, God promises to release His power in answer to prayer.

Interestingly, this is what happened in Jerusalem. After the disciples had "raised their voices together in prayer to God . . . the place where they were meeting was shaken" (Acts 4:24-31). Though God's power was uniquely revealed in the early days of the church in ways that we would not expect to be normative throughout church history, God still is the *omnipotent* God. He's still in the business of answering prayer. He still wants to reveal His power in our midst. Furthermore, He has made the condition clear—lifting our voices together as *one* body, reflecting oneness of heart and soul.

Unity, God's Power, and Answered Prayer in the Church Today

Throughout history, Satan has attempted to destroy unity among Christians because he knows that oneness of heart and mind releases God's power in various ways, but particularly through answered prayer. Consequently, Satan is ever on the lookout for a chink in our armor. When he finds it, he does all he can to drive a wedge between and among Christians.

But we need not fear Satan. He *can* be defeated. He need not win the battle. It is possible to maintain unity and to experience God's power, particularly through answered prayer. To do so, however, we must faithfully follow God's game plan:

We must follow the example of Jesus Christ and of the Apostle Paul and pray for unity (Eph. 6:18). In this sense prayer is a means to unity and unity is a *means* to answered prayer.

We must be obedient to Christ and follow the way of love, doing all we can to maintain unity (John 15:17; 1 Cor. 14:1). Though we should pray for unity, we are responsible to cooperate with God in creating that unity.

We must methodically follow God's procedure if someone sins against us (Matt. 18:15-17). This is a clear example of how Christians are responsible to maintain unity. Furthermore, this represents the primary way to keep Satan from getting his foot in the door. Probably 99 percent of all problems of disunity in the church (and family) could be solved if Christians obeyed Christ's teaching in Matthew 18:15-17.

We must forgive those who sin against us (Matt. 18:21-22; Col. 3:13). There can be no unity without forgiveness. Again, this is a Christian's responsibility. It is to be an act of the will, a decisive action.

No matter what happens, we must not allow anger and bitterness to continue in our lives (Eph. 4:32). To continue with an unforgiving spirit will eventually result in a root of bitterness. Again, Satan can use this condition to eat away at unity in the church.

It is at this point that leaders in the church must take Paul's teaching on this subject very seriously. A bitter, angry person is trapped in sin and needs help. Thus, Paul wrote:

Brothers, if someone is caught in a sin, you who are spiritual should restore him gently. But watch yourself, or you also may be tempted. Carry each other's burdens, and in this way you will fulfill the law of Christ (Gal. 6:1-2).

On one occasion I was invited to speak at a missionary conference in Quito, Ecuador. Before the conference began, I was speaking with one of the missionary couples who had worked with an Indian tribe for a number of years. The missionary wife reflected on a revival that broke out in the tribe a number of years before, resulting in thousands of conversions to Christ. Not knowing that I was going to speak on the subject of unity and how God uses that condition to reveal His power, she said, "It was at that very time there was a spirit of unity among the missionary leaders that we had never experienced before."

As I listened to her story, my heart was deeply moved. She was verifying experientially the very thing I was going to speak about. God's power *was* released through the oneness of heart and soul that existed among those missionary leaders. When they confessed their sins to one another and forgave one another and restored love and unity, God's Spirit moved through them to reach thousands of Indians for Jesus Christ.

A Challenge

Check your own life. Are you in violation of any of the spiritual guidelines mentioned in this chapter? Could this be why God is not answering your prayers or the prayers of your church?

If you are out of God's will, ask the Lord to help you be obedient to Him. If personal and private prayer does not seem to be helping you overcome your problems, then *remember what Jesus said:* "Again, I tell you that if two of you on earth agree about anything you ask for, it will be done for you by My Father in heaven" (Matt. 18:19).

Father, I pray that You will preserve unity in my church. Reveal to me any areas where I am not following the way of love. If I have been truly offended by anyone, help me to follow Your divine procedure. Help me never to criticize another Christian who has sinned against me without going to that person first. Lord, reveal to me if what I consider an offense is really more my problem than the other person's. Help me to always have a forgiving spirit. Help me never to allow bitterness and anger to grip my soul.

A Project
If you have difficulty with bitterness toward another Christian, begin by praying for that person every day. Ask God to bring healing to that person and to your own heart.

NOTE: To seek advice from a mature Christian about dealing with the offense is certainly not inappropriate. However, criticizing another person without dealing with the offense according to God's procedure *is* a violation of His will.

6

God's Providence

In Ken Boa's book *God, I Don't Understand!* (Victor), he raises a number of perplexing questions:
- How can Jesus be both God and man?
- How can God dwell in eternity and yet act in time?
- How can the Bible be both divine and human in origin?
- How can God be three Persons and yet one God?
- How can God be sovereign and man still free to choose?

We could add another question to this list:
- *How can prayer be reconciled with God's providence?*

The word *providence* is not used in the Bible. However, like the word *trinity,* it represents a biblical doctrine and is frequently illustrated in the Scriptures.

Some Formal Definitions
Before we look at how this concept is illustrated in Scripture and especially in the context of prayer, let's look at some formal definitions.

Dr. Lewis Sperry Chafer, founder and first president of Dallas Theological Seminary, stated, "Providence is the execution in all its detail of the divine program of the ages" (*Systematic Theology,* vol. 1, Dallas Seminary Press, p. 44).

Dr. Augustine Strong, a great Baptist theologian, said, "Providence is that continuous agency of God by which He makes all the events of the physical and moral universe fulfill the original design with which He created it" (*Systematic Theology,* Judson Press, p. 419).

J. Oliver Bushwell, a well-known Lutheran theologian, wrote, "God is not only the Creator of all things, but He continuously sustains and rules all His creation" (*A Systematic Theology of the Christian Religion,* Zondervan, p. 170).

T.H.L. Parker defines this concept more practically. "The doctrine of providence tells us that the world and our lives are not ruled by chance or by fate but by God" (Everett S. Harrison, ed., *Baker's Dictionary of Theology,* Baker, p. 427).

If these definitions are biblically accurate (and I believe they are), how does prayer fit into God's sovereign and providential plans? Someone might argue that if God has planned everything and if the plan is going to be fulfilled, why pray at all? If God has planned certain things, won't they happen anyway?

The best way to answer questions like these is to look at the examples from New Testament Christians. How did they resolve this problem?

A New Testament Example

In chapter 5 we reviewed a New Testament prayer meeting in Jerusalem. Peter and John had just been released from jail. After reporting on their experiences while they were held in custody, the believers all "raised their voices together in prayer to God." With one mind and in unity they joined their hearts in prayer. From this example and other passages of Scripture we observed that unity among Christians is a basic condition set forth in Scripture for God to release His power to answer prayer. The specific prayer itself, however, illustrates the subject of this chapter

First, these believers addressed God as their "Sovereign Lord"—the One who has "made the heaven and the earth and the sea, and everything in them" (Acts 4:24).

We quickly discover, however, that these Christians had more in mind than God's creative power in nature. They next mentioned God's special revelation to David. Quoting Psalm 2:1-2 in their prayer, they said:

> You spoke by the Holy Spirit through the mouth of Your servant, our father David: "Why do the nations rage and the peoples plot in vain? The kings of the earth take their stand and the rulers gather together against the Lord and against His anointed one" (Acts 4:25-26).

Next, their prayer interprets exactly what David really meant.

> Indeed Herod and Pontius Pilate met together with the Gentiles and the people of Israel in the city to conspire against Your holy servant Jesus, whom You anointed. They did what Your power and will had decided beforehand should happen (vv. 27-28).

The most difficult statement to understand in this prayer is in verse 28. There we see that what men did in crucifying Jesus Christ was already predetermined. These men were simply carrying out the plan of God in crucifying Jesus. It's at this point we can become confused regarding God's sovereign plan and human freedom.

Three Observations

First, these Christians believed in God's providence—and yet they prayed! They did not allow their belief in a sovereign God who controls and directs the affairs of mankind to interfere with their human responsibility to pray.

Second, these Christians believed that God answered prayer—and that prayer indeed made a difference! This is why they asked God for two specific requests:

> Now, Lord, consider their threats and enable Your servants *to speak Your Word with great boldness* (4:29).

> Stretch out Your hand *to heal* and *perform miraculous signs and wonders* through the name of Your holy servant Jesus (v. 30).

Third, God answered their prayer. Thus we read—"After they prayed, the place where they were meeting *was shaken.* And they were all filled with the Holy Spirit and *spoke the Word of God boldly"* (v. 31). In other words, God continued to work miracles and He enabled them to speak out boldly for Jesus Christ in spite of the threats from the religious leaders.

There are many other biblical examples where Christians recognized God's sovereignty. There are also many examples where Christians prayed and asked God to intervene in everyday affairs—and He did! They did not allow the great truth of God's providence to interfere with the privilege God gave them to come into His presence and request help in every time of need.

Prayer *does* make a difference. Biblical history and church history are filled with illustrations of this truth. However, while at home on this earth, we will never understand completely how answers to prayer can be reconciled with the fixity of natural law and the eternal decree and foreknowledge of God. For example, if God has decreed or foreseen that a sickness would result in death, or that any other event would occur, how could man's prayer in any way alter the outcome? How can this be? We can only answer, "God, we don't understand! But we believe it is possible!"

A Biblical Antinomy

In trying to reconcile God's providence and prayer we are dealing with an incomprehensible concept. There are many such concepts in Scripture.

Ken Boa calls these incomprehensible mysteries antinomies (*God, I Don't Understand,* Victor, pp. 14-15). Webster defines an antinomy as "a contradiction between two apparently equally valid principles." Though they appear paradoxical, both are true. At this point, we *can't* understand completely because we are dealing with God's infinite revelation which often takes us *far beyond* the limits of our human intelligence. Where our understanding ends, God's begins.

What happens when we try to explain a biblical antinomy?

We end up going to two extremes. We try to remove the tension by ignoring one truth or the other. This often leads to confusion, disappointment, and disillusionment. And in other instances, it leads to outright doctrinal error.

Related to prayer, if we do not accept the tension, we may make demands of God—and be disappointed when He doesn't answer. Or, we may become fatalistic and refuse to pray because we conclude "that what will be will be." At other times we may ask God to do things without seeking His will and then proceed to try and make things happen with our own human efforts.

Some Biblical Guidelines

Though there are many mysteries that we do not understand (which is part of the marvel of the Christian faith), it is important that we function in the light of what we *do* understand. Regarding prayer, God has given us some very specific and understandable guidelines.

1. God responds when Christians pray together in love and unity. This we have already observed in the previous chapter. In some miraculous way, God releases His power when Christians lift their voices to Him with one heart and mind. Let us follow Christ's example as well as Paul's and pray for this unity. Let us follow the biblical exhortation to always "make every effort to keep the unity of the Spirit through the bond of peace" (Eph. 4:3).

2. God responds when we pray in faith, but according to His will. John made this point clear in his first epistle: "This is the assurance we have in approaching God: that if we ask anything *according to His will,* He hears us. And if we know that He hears us—whatever we ask—we know that we have what we ask of Him" (1 John 5:14-15).

As Christians, then, we must always seek to ask for things that are in harmony with God's will for our lives. The only sure way of knowing God's will is to understand more and more of His revealed Word. When believers join their hearts together around common scriptural wisdom, they can truly pray "in the Spirit" (Eph. 6:18), and "according to His will" (1 John 5:14).

How does this work out practically? Many times I have joined other elders in the church praying for someone who is ill. When leading this special prayer service, I have always tried to point out that we do not know what God's will is regarding healing. We *do* know that God is all-powerful. We *do* know that on occasions throughout biblical history He has miraculously healed people. We *do* know He can do anything He wants—even raising the dead. But we also know that God did not always answer this kind of prayer, even when it was voiced by one of His choicest servants.

Paul stands out as a superb example. God used this man to heal many people. But there came a time in Paul's own life when he too suffered from a serious physical affliction. Paul called this problem a "thorn" in his "flesh." Writing to the Corinthians, he said—"Three times I pleaded with the Lord to take it away from me." The Lord did not answer Paul's prayer with physical healing. Instead, He reminded Paul that His "grace was sufficient" to help Paul bear this burden. "My power is made perfect in weakness," He reassured His servant (2 Cor. 12:8-9).

There are Christians who teach that it is *always* God's will to heal people when they pray. If this were true, why didn't God answer Paul's prayer? And also, if this were true, there would be the potential that people would never die from physical deterioration. This, of course, is illogical and absurd. Scripture makes it clear that this kind of "praying" is not according to the will of God.

On the other hand, it *may be* God's will to heal. Therefore, we should pray *in faith,* believing that God can heal if He so chooses. In many instances, He does. But if He doesn't, like Paul, we must accept God's response and not blame ourselves or others for lack of faith. To violate this truth at times heaps guilt on people that is far more devastating than the physical illness itself.

On one occasion my wife and I were watching a Christian "healer" on television. A small child was sitting in the front row obviously very ill with a serious form of physical retardation due to brain damage. From all appearances there was no mental retardation, so the child seemed to clearly comprehend what was being said.

The man's statements were typical. "If you believe, God will heal you! Do you believe this?"

The child nodded approval and assent with the most sincere expression I've ever seen. Then the healer prayed, encouraging the audience to believe that God was going to heal the child. But, predictably, nothing happened.

As I watched the expression on the child's face, my heart was torn. At this point, that little boy had an additional burden to bear—the constant thought that he did not have enough faith to be healed, or that the people in the audience did not take God seriously.

How tragic! There is no question that God could have healed that child *if* it was His will. But no doubt it was not His will. If the man praying for the child knew the Scriptures, as he should, he would not have led that child—and the audience—into a false hope and into false guilt. This is why it is so important that we understand what God says so that we can indeed pray according to His will.

Before we leave this point, let's look at another important fact. We know that it *is* God's will to provide grace to a Christian who is bearing a burden. This is why God told Paul that His grace was sufficient for him, even though He did not remove the physical difficulty. Thus, we too, can always pray that God will comfort the downhearted and provide help in every trial and problem. We do not need to pray, "If it be Your will, Lord," when we ask for comfort in the midst of trials. We already *know* it is the will of God to do so (Phil. 4:6-7).

3. God responds to unselfish prayers. James made this point clear in his letter to Jewish Christians who were scattered throughout the New Testament world. "When you ask," he wrote, "you do not receive, because you ask with *wrong motives,* that you may spend what you get on *your pleasures*" (James 4:3).

God does not promise to respond to prayers that are selfish. Consequently, we must always search our hearts. *Why* are we praying? Are *our* desires *His* desires?

For example, we may be praying for a better economic situation. However, are we truly in harmony in our hearts with what Jesus said? "But seek first His kingdom and His righteousness, and all these things will be given to you as well" (Matt. 6:33).

This is a deep question, and one we need lots of time to think through and experience. Remember that God cannot be manipulated by superficial responses. He knows our hearts, even when we do not. In order to reveal our true motives, He sometimes allows what appears to us to be rather long periods of time to really come to know ourselves. We must not be impatient with God, for if we are, we have already revealed our motives.

4. *God responds to prayer in special ways on special occasions and at special times in order to achieve His sovereign purposes.* The Scriptures illustrate vividly that there are various periods of time in history when God acts sovereignly to achieve His purpose. Often this has been related to miraculous signs and wonders, both in *response* to prayer—and *apart* from prayer.

A letter to the Hebrew Christians illustrates this point. After reminding us that God has spoken "in these last days" by sending His Son into the world, the writer explains how God convinced people that what Jesus taught was true. "This salvation, which was first announced by the Lord, was confirmed to us by those who heard Him. God also testified to it by signs, wonders, and various miracles, and gifts of the Holy Spirit *distributed according to His will*" (Heb. 2:3-4).

This is what was happening in the early part of the Book of Acts. In response to prayer, God revealed Himself in unusual and powerful ways, just as He enabled Jesus to verify His message with miracles.

God has not promised to always confirm His message in this way. Biblical history illustrates this. In fact, there are two very significant, but brief, periods of time out of thousands of years of history that God's "silence" was broken with supernatural miracles and wonders. The first was when God revealed His

Law to Israel. He did so with great and miraculous manifestations. The actual miracles at Mount Sinai were also preceded by the great demonstrations of His power in Egypt and at the Red Sea. When God finally spoke to Moses and gave him the Ten Commandments, it was in the context of incredible supernatural phenomena. God was *confirming* His spoken and written message. He did not want His people to miss the fact that His message was indeed authoritative and supernatural.

The second period of time relates to the New Testament period. It began primarily with Jesus Christ. In fact, God had not spoken directly with any man for nearly 400 years. He broke this silence when He spoke to Zacharias in the temple and announced the birth of John the Baptist, the forerunner of Jesus Christ. Then God revealed Himself directly through the birth of Christ and His later teaching ministry. God confirmed Jesus' message of salvation "by signs, wonders, and various miracles" (Heb. 2:4).

When Jesus returned to heaven, He continued that process through the apostles, particularly till the New Testament was written. Thus He confirmed His message "to us by those who heard" Jesus teach. Again He verified this message by "signs, wonders, and various miracles." Thus we read in the Book of Acts that as the New Testament Christians "devoted themselves to the apostles' teaching and to the fellowship and to breaking of bread and to prayer . . . many wonders and marvelous signs were done *by the apostles*" (Acts 2:42-43).

We cannot expect God to duplicate these miracles at will throughout church history. He could, if He wanted to. He is still the omnipotent God. But it is clear He has not chosen to do this on a regular basis. This does not mean He will not at times work in miraculous ways, but we must always "pray in His will." That is why it is so important that we understand what His will actually is. We must emphasize the most important way that we can be sure of His will is through the written Word of God which He has communicated to us and verified "by signs, wonders, and various miracles, and gifts of the Holy Spirit *distributed according to His will*."

5. *God responds to prayer with answers that are best for us.*
God is presented in Scripture as a loving, heavenly Father and
we are His children. Since He is omniscient, He knows what is
best for every one of us.

As earthly parents we should be able to understand this
concept. There are times when we say no to our children when
they make requests because we know what they are asking is
not best for them. In fact, it may ultimately bring them severe
hurt, disappointment, and pain. Even with our inferior knowledge, we generally know what is best for our children. But
remember, our heavenly Father *always* knows what is best. He
wouldn't be a loving Father if He allowed us to have things that
are destructive.

If your 3-year-old begged you for a sharp knife to play with,
would you give it to him? What if your "mature" 14-year-old
asked if he could use the family car to drive a group of his
friends to the beach? Would you let him? Of course not—not
if you love your son or daughter. Neither will God give us things
we ask for that will hurt us or destroy us.

Charles Conn in his book entitled, *Making It Happen,* states
this concept very well.

> God's timing is always better than ours. He brings us
> along slowly and skillfully. We get impatient. We
> want it all now. Sometimes we set goals that may be
> good goals, worthy goals, but which we are not ready
> to handle. When we do, it only makes sense that a
> loving Father will keep those things out of our reach.
>
> Only God knows what might be the implication for
> your overall well-being if you become famous or
> wealthy, if you married that girl, got that promotion,
> cut that hit record, or simply could afford to move to
> that neighborhood you've always wanted to live in.
> He knows.
>
> And part of what it means to be God's children is
> to accept that He knows and that He will help bring
> what is really best into our lives—not what we want
> every time, but what is really best for us (Revell, pp.
> 85-86).

A Challenge

There are actually three thoughts that emerge from this chapter that help in understanding prayer and God's providence. Two of these relate to the actual prayer in Acts 4. The third relates to the whole of Scripture.

First, do I recognize God as the sovereign Lord of the universe? Do I live my life realizing that He is in control? Do I believe this great truth, even though I do not understand it?

Second, even though God is sovereign, do I use the freedom that God has given me to pray and ask for help? Do I believe that prayer really makes a difference?

Third, do I pray according to the guidelines God has made clear and understandable?

• Am I getting together with other mature Christians and praying about mutual needs in love and unity?

• Am I seeking God's will in the Word of God so I can pray accordingly?

• Am I praying unselfishly?

• Do I realize that God responds in different ways and in different times according to His sovereign will, thus explaining why all biblical answers to prayer are not considered to be a normative experience for Christians of all time?

• Do I view God as a loving heavenly Father, who responds to my prayers in a way that is best for me?

> *Father, I acknowledge my human limitations. I don't understand how You are a sovereign God and yet You respond to my prayers. But I'm thankful that You do answer when I pray according to Your divine guidelines.*

A Project

Read Paul's letter to the Ephesians. How does Paul's faith in God's sovereign plans for His children affect his view of prayer?

7

A Pastoral Priority

The church in Jerusalem experienced phenomenal growth (see Figure 2). Beginning with 120 people in the first Upper Room prayer meeting (Acts 1:15), this number quickly exploded to about 3,000 (2:41). The coming of the Holy Spirit on the Day of Pentecost, accompanied by marvelous signs and wonders, plus Peter's dynamic sermon which interpreted these events, convinced thousands of Jews that Jesus Christ was indeed the true Messiah. From that point forward their numbers increased daily as people became exposed to this new community of love and reality (v. 45).

The growth phenomena in the Jerusalem church can also be explained by the "principle of readiness." The majority of these first converts were Jews who had been looking for the Messiah. Jerusalem was also one of the focal areas for Jesus' earthly teaching and healing ministry. When this great body of people recognized that Jesus was indeed the Christ they had been looking for, they had responded en masse.

The results of the Christian movement were predictable. Jewish leaders who were responsible for Christ's death were greatly threatened. What they had attempted to destroy and thwart was only gaining momentum. Furthermore, thousands of their own followers were becoming converts to Christianity.

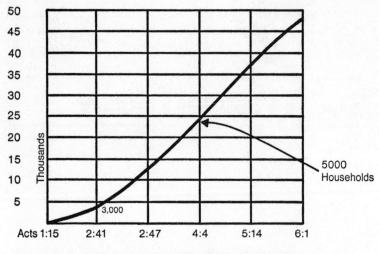

GROWTH IN THE JERUSALEM CHURCH

Figure 2

They countered by arresting Peter and John, who had become primary spokesmen for this new movement. But by this time the church had grown to what appears to be "about 5,000 households" (4:4).

Many Bible interpreters believe the reference to "5,000 men" actually refers to 5,000 households. If each household comprised 5 individuals, the church would have already grown to include 25,000 people. However, since the "extended family" was normative in the New Testament world including servants, some households would have numbered far more than those included in the typical nuclear family.

As persecution has demonstrated so often, it only intensified interest in the Christian message. Added to this impetus were the miraculous signs and wonders that the apostles continued to perform. Following the awesome events involving Ananias and Sapphira, Luke records that "all the more believers in the Lord, *multitudes* of men and women, were constantly added to their number" (5:14, NASB).

Again there was a counter-movement by the religious leaders in Jerusalem. This time they jailed *all* the apostles, seemingly unaware that they were engaged in a supernatural struggle. The Lord miraculously delivered these evangelists, sending an angel that night to open the prison gates. As the angel released them, he said, "Go, stand in the temple courts . . . and tell the people the full message of this new life" (v. 20).

You can imagine their surprise when the Jewish leaders found the apostles missing and discovered them back in the temple teaching that Jesus Christ was truly the Messiah. Had they been open at all, they would have thought twice before they once again took the apostles into custody. However, emotion often overrides rational thinking. Once again taking them captive, the Jewish leaders ordered them to stop teaching about Jesus Christ. At this point Peter uttered his classic statement which has served as a motivating force for persecuted Christians down through the centuries. "We must," he said, "obey God rather than men" (v. 29).

This statement only angered the religious leaders even more. Some wanted to take the apostles' lives immediately. However, those who were more rational knew that this kind of violent behavior would bring negative results among the followers of Christ who were increasing by the thousands. Therefore, they decided to flog the apostles and warn them once again not to speak in the name of Jesus Christ.

But their warning was to no avail. Following their release, the apostles with ever increasing boldness, "never stopped teaching and proclaiming the Good News that Jesus is the Christ" (v. 42). And the church kept right on growing.

The Problems of Growth

Numerical growth in any community of people always creates difficulties of one sort or another. The church is not exempt. As numbers increase, so do human needs. Sooner or later someone is going to be neglected. Communication breakdowns occur. If steps are not taken to correct the situation, the problems will get worse.

The First Problem (Acts 6:1). It should not surprise us that this very thing occurred in Jerusalem. "In those days," Luke records, "when the number of disciples *was increasing,* the Grecian Jews among them complained against those of the Aramaic-speaking community because their widows were being overlooked in the daily distribution of food" (v. 1).

Why was this happening? Who were the "Grecian Jews" and who were the people who made up the "Aramaic-speaking community"? Why this tension?

To understand this problem, we must remember that Jews had come from all over the New Testament world for a special 50-day festival (2:5). It was on the first day—the Day of Pentecost—that the Holy Spirit descended on a small group of Christ's disciples, giving birth to the church. A crowd quickly gathered and people heard the name of God declared in numerous languages.

In conjunction with this event, many of those who responded to Peter's message stayed in Jerusalem rather than return to their own countries. Too much was happening in Jerusalem to leave. With their limited knowledge of Christ's future plans, they no doubt thought that He would return within days to set up His kingdom.

To care for these people, many believing Jews who lived in Jerusalem and its environs (the Aramaic-speaking community) sold "their possessions and goods" and "gave to anyone who had need" (v. 45). For awhile this rather spontaneous system worked. Needs were met, people were cared for, "and the Lord added to their number daily those who were being saved" (v. 47).

But *growth* of this nature always outgrows spontaneity. So it happened in Jerusalem. Some of the widows who were among those who had come from other countries were being neglected when food was distributed in this semi-communal society.

The Second Problem (6:2). This kind of pressure always generates a second problem. Those who were primary leaders in this growing Christian community were faced with an overload of responsibilities. In most instances, if leaders don't face this kind of difficulty and solve it organizationally, they'll end up getting their own priorities out of order.

A Solution (vv. 3-6). The apostles faced this very problem. However, they show how to solve it.

First, they refused to get sidetracked from their primary responsibilities. For them it involved teaching the Word of God and giving themselves to prayer (vv. 2, 4). "It would not be right," they reported to the people (v. 2). They *knew* what their priorities were.

Second, they proposed a concrete solution. "Brothers," they said, "choose seven men from among you who are known to be full of the Spirit and wisdom. We will turn this responsibility over to them and will give our attention to *prayer* and the *ministry of the Word*" (vv. 3-4).

With this statement, the apostles were also taking a third step. They informed everyone what their God-ordained priorities were, and that they dared not get sidetracked into other areas, as important as those areas might be.

Fourth, they outlined for these New Testament Christians another important factor. To avoid getting their own priorities out of focus, they needed to *delegate* responsibility to other *qualified* people.

Luke reports that "this proposal pleased the whole group." Consequently, they chose seven capable men to care for the neglected widows.

The Results (v. 7). The results of facing this problem squarely and resolving it are also very significant. It represents the true test as to whether a solution is satisfactory. "The Word of God spread. The number of disciples in Jerusalem increased rapidly, and a large number of priests became obedient to the faith" (v. 7).

In many respects this biblical account ends where it began. The church was growing! Growth brought problems. The apostles resolved the problem without getting sidetracked from their own God-given priorities. And the church kept right on growing!

This is a very important observation. Some 20th-century Christians try to solve church growth problems by stopping growth. To do so is to contradict the whole message and intent of Christianity. The church that does so will eventually self-destruct. It will turn inward and grow sour. There can be no status quo and be what God intends the church to be.

On the other hand, some 20th-century church leaders resolve church growth problems by becoming enmeshed in the problems themselves, trying to do everything. They end up doing nothing well. Even more unfortunately, they get away from their biblical priorities; namely, teaching the Word of God faithfully and giving themselves to prayer. When that happens the church begins to suffer serious internal weaknesses.

When spiritual leaders try to do everything themselves, and do nothing well, they grow increasingly frustrated and eventually become exhausted. Again, their work deteriorates. Of course, this approach does not meet people's needs. When people's needs are not met, the work suffers even more deterioration.

An Old Testament Example

Moses faced a situation similar to that of the apostles when he led the Children of Israel out of Egypt. The sheer size of this great company of people—nearly 2 million plus—would be awesome for any leader. When this is combined with the problems encountered traveling through wilderness territory, plus the people's spiritual immaturity, we can better understand the gigantic task Moses faced.

The Problem (Ex. 18:13-18). One day while Israel was camped in the wilderness, Moses was seated in a special place where people could ask his counsel for solving various problems. His father-in-law Jethro, who had come to visit Moses, was watching and listening. He immediately sensed Moses was in trouble. There was no way Moses could handle the multitude of problems of all of these people. "The work is too heavy for you!" Jethro exclaimed. "You cannot handle it alone" (Ex. 18:18).

The Solution (vv. 19-23). Jethro encouraged Moses to establish his priorities and then to devise a plan to meet the people's needs. "You must be the people's representative before God and bring their disputes to Him," advised Jethro. "Teach them the decrees and laws, and show them the way to live and the duties they are to perform" (vv. 19-20).

Jethro then advised Moses to delegate some of his responsibilities to others. Note carefully what kind of men they were to be: "Select *capable* men from all the people—men who *fear God, trustworthy* men who *hate dishonest gain*—and appoint them as officials over thousands, hundreds, fifties, and tens" (v. 21).

These men were to handle the simpler problems; the more difficult problems would still be directed to Moses.

The Results (vv. 24-27). Moses followed Jethro's advice with God's blessing. And it worked. Moses was able to survive physically and emotionally. The peoples' needs were met. God's plan for Israel proceeded on schedule.

Supra-Cultural Principles

There are two important supra-cultural principles in both of these New Testament and Old Testament stories.

First, Christian leaders must *establish biblical priorities.* Those priorities are clearly enunciated. Though Moses lived and served God in a different setting, he was still to have a teaching and prayer ministry among the people. So were the apostles. In both situations, these leaders were in danger of getting involved in activities—important activities—that would keep them from carrying out their priority functions.

Second, Christian leaders should solve problems by *appointing qualified leaders* to help them. In both biblical illustrations, the leaders involved had to share the responsibility of leadership. But in both cases, they shared it with *capable* individuals. To appoint unqualified leaders would have doubled their trouble and sidetracked them even more from their priorities.

Church Leaders Today

It is clear from this biblical overview that there is continuity in God's plan for leadership (see Figure 3). In Acts 6, the church was becoming established. The apostles were laying the foundation. Later, elders or bishops were appointed to manage individ-

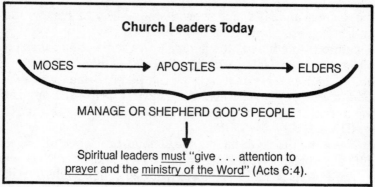

Figure 3

ual local churches. Interestingly, these were the first spiritual leaders appointed by Paul and Barnabas as they returned to visit the churches that were founded on the first missionary journey (Acts 14:21-23).

The titles *elders* and *bishops* were used interchangeably in the New Testament period. The word *elder* comes from the Jewish community and the word *bishop* from the Greek and Roman communities. The use of these words in the New Testament illustrates cultural adaptation, since the word *bishop* is used only in those churches that were heavily populated with converts from the Gentile world (the churches at Ephesus, Philippi, and Crete).

Scripture makes it clear that elders are *to manage* or shepherd the flock of God (1 Tim. 3:4-5; Acts 20:28; 1 Peter 5:2-3). *Managing* or *shepherding* represents a very comprehensive function. *Managing* is a concrete term and describes responsibility for the general supervision of the church. *Shepherding* is a more illustrative term, comparing the management responsibilities for the church to a shepherd who pastors a flock of sheep. Jesus used this term to describe His own role when He referred to Himself as the "Good Shepherd" and to us as "His sheep" (John 10:11).

The "shepherd" or "pastoral" concept is a very beautiful

and appropriate way to describe an elder's leadership role. It adds a dimension that the word *managing* does not fully convey. Though *managing* describes overall leadership responsibility, the term *shepherding* or *pastoring* describes what this managing responsibility involves.

Any shepherd has two basic responsibilities. First, he must "*feed* the flock;" secondly, he must "*care* for the flock." These words describe the priorities of any spiritual leader, as illustrated by both Moses and the apostles. We must "feed" Christians with the Word of God. "Caring" certainly involves prayer as a primary means of meeting needs. Thus James wrote, "Is any one of you sick? He should call for the elders of the church to pray over him and anoint him with oil in the name of the Lord" (James 5:14). Perhaps James, when he suggests anointing with oil, is drawing from David's analogy of his Great Shepherd, "You anoint my head with oil" (Ps. 23:5). This certainly describes what a good shepherd does when one of his sheep is wounded or hurt. Perhaps James is also drawing on Christ's Parable of the Good Samaritan, who finding a man beaten and hurt "bandaged his wounds, pouring on *oil* and wine" (Luke 10:34).

Prayer and teaching the Word of God are certainly pastoral priorities. Though all Christians are to pray for one another and teach one another, spiritual leaders have a special, God-ordained responsibility to give themselves to prayer and to the ministry of the Word. However, there are many *good* activities in the church that tend to sidetrack elders away from this responsibility. People have many legitimate needs that often take pastoral time. But there is no greater need than prayer and teaching the Word of God.

There is only one way to solve this problem. Like Moses and the apostles, spiritual leaders today must establish prayer and the ministry of the Word as priorities. They must let the people know that these are priorities and that they won't be sidetracked away from them.

To keep from getting distracted, spiritual leaders must delegate responsibility to qualified people to help them—first, more qualified shepherds to care for the pastoral needs of people; and secondly, to appoint qualified people to care for other kinds of needs in the church. Scripture designates these people as deacons and/or deaconesses (1 Tim. 3:8-11). This certainly describes the men who were appointed by the apostles to care for the needy widows in the growing Jerusalem church.

We must remember that those appointed *must* be qualified. This is why Paul clearly outlines the qualifications for elders *and* deacons and deaconesses (vv. 1-13). Elders were to pastor and teach. Deacons and deaconesses were to help care for all other needs in the church. But both kinds of leaders were to be spiritually qualified.

When these principles are followed, God's Word will prosper. Needs will be met. The church will maintain unity and many will come to know Jesus Christ and be added to the church—just as was true in the New Testament world.

A Challenge

When I first shared this message with a group of Christians in Dallas, we had just launched a new Fellowship Bible Church. This church represented 10 such churches that had come into existence in the Dallas community during the last several years. At that particular time we were experiencing unusual growth in this new church and, in essence, facing some of the same challenges experienced by the apostles in Jerusalem. Though our numbers were in no way comparable, the dynamics certainly were.

That Sunday morning, as I shared this message, I challenged the people to pray in three areas:

1. That as we grew as a church, we'd make sure people's total needs were met.
2. That as we grew as a church, we—as spiritual leaders— would keep our priorities in focus.
3. That as we grew as a church, we'd keep these priorities in focus by equipping and appointing spiritually qualified leaders.

What about your church? To what extent are you applying

these supra-cultural principles? The following "satisfaction" scale will help you evaluate your situation.

	Dissatis-faction	Satis-faction
Are we meeting people's total needs with proper organizational structures?	1 2 3 4 5 6	7 8 9 10
Are spiritual leaders keeping their priorities straight by giving proper time to teaching the Word and prayer?	1 2 3 4 5 6	7 8 9 10
Are we equipping and appointing qualified leaders to enable our pastors and elders to maintain their priorities?	1 2 3 4 5 6	7 8 9 10

Dear Father, help the members in my church to be aware of people's total needs. May we not ignore them. But, Father, don't allow the physical and emotional needs of people to sidetrack our spiritual leaders from maintaining their priorities to teach Your Word and to spend time in prayer. We ask that You'll help us equip and produce qualified men and women in the church who will assist our pastors in doing Your work.

A Project
In a spirit of deep love and concern, ask your pastor (or pastors) to read this chapter and give you an evaluation of its content. Ask them also to share with you if they feel other members of the body of Christ are doing their part in assisting them in the ministry so that they might maintain their biblical priority.

8

Peter's Prison Experience

Prologue

The popularity and growth of the church in Jerusalem eventually led to all-out persecution. Triggered by Stephen's martyrdom and Saul's intense desire to destroy the church, the Jerusalem Christians "were scattered throughout Judea and Samaria" (Acts 8:1). In fact, we read that "all except the apostles" left Jerusalem (v. 1).

Imagine this great company of believers. Multiplied thousands left Jerusalem and "preached the Word wherever they went" (v. 4). God's plans were on schedule, in spite of the fact that most wanted to stay in Jerusalem and enjoy the good things that were happening in the early days of the church. But Jesus had said, "You will be My witnesses in Jerusalem, *and* in all Judea and Samaria, *and* to the ends of the earth" (1:8). Persecution became the means whereby believers were obedient to Christ's command.

But persecution eventually subsided, particularly after Saul was converted on the road to Damascus. "The church throughout Judea, Galilee, and Samaria enjoyed a time of peace" (9:31). Christians could travel rather freely sharing their faith.

However, their growing presence was still threatening and continued to create opposition among Jewish leaders. Herod

Agrippa I had become king over Judea and Samaria, which made him "king of the Jews." Politically motivated, he prided himself in being a "friend" of the Jews, even supporting their laws and customs.

Peter's Arrest (Acts 12:1-4)

Because Herod was so obsessed with self-glory and political ambition, he saw the growing Jewish-Christian conflict and tension as an opportunity to ingratiate himself even more with the Jewish community. He selected certain key Christian leaders and had them thrown into prison. Among them was the Apostle James, John's brother. Herod's ruthless character was revealed when he had James executed.

Though the Jewish leaders themselves were not leading out in persecution, they were delighted when Herod moved into the arena. No doubt working behind the scenes, they affirmed Herod's hideous actions against James. This, in turn, appealed to the king's oversized ego and he decided to go after the leading spokesman for Christianity ever since Pentecost—the Apostle Peter. If Herod could make the Jewish community happy by taking James' life, he knew he would score high if he could do the same with the Apostle Peter.

Herod's insecurity in taking this step became obvious when he ordered Peter to be guarded "by four squads of four soldiers each" (12:4). Why 16 men to guard a fisherman turned preacher? Herod knew he was not dealing with an ordinary movement or ordinary people. There was every evidence that something supernatural was taking place. This was not the first time one of the apostles had been arrested and put in jail. On one occasion the apostles had been miraculously released from jail by an angel of the Lord. The next day their accusers discovered them teaching God's Word in the temple (5:17-21). This time Herod was taking no chances.

The Church at Prayer (Acts 12:5)

At this juncture, the Jerusalem Christians were deeply concerned James had already been executed. Now Peter's life was also in danger. They knew Herod would stop at nothing. So they did the only thing they could do—they gathered together and prayed earnestly for Peter (12:5).

Luke does not tell us the content of their prayers. However, from the overall story as it is told by Luke, we can conclude that they evidently were *not* praying for a miraculous delivery. They realized that James had *not* been released or protected from Herod's evil sword. They could only conclude that Peter was next.

What did they pray? Perhaps they asked the Lord for *protection*—hoping that in some way Herod would have mercy. Perhaps they prayed that Peter might have *boldness* to face his persecutors without wavering in his faith, even if it meant death. Jesus, of course, had foretold that many of His men would suffer severe persecution. In fact, Jesus had spoken specifically regarding the death that Peter would die (John 21:18). It would be surprising if Peter had not shared this at some point with his fellow Christians in Jerusalem, perhaps even in connection with his present imprisonment. Thus, they would not be surprised that this might be the time that Peter's life would be taken.

The apostles were prepared to die for Christ. They knew this would eventually happen—at least for most of them—and indeed it did. As far as we know, tradition tells us the Apostle John was the only one who died a natural death.

The Apostle Paul also knew death was always a strong possibility. This was reflected in his letter to the Philippians, written while he was in prison in Rome. He did not know whether he would be executed or released, but he wrote, "I know that through your prayers and the help given by the Spirit of Jesus Christ, what has happened to me will turn out for my deliverance" (Phil. 1:19).

By *deliverance* Paul did not mean release from prison, though he did not exclude that possibility. Rather, he meant that no matter what the outcome, he wanted to stand firm for Christ. Thus he wrote, "I eagerly expect and hope that I will in no way *be ashamed*, but will have sufficient *courage* so that now as always Christ will be exalted in my body, whether by life or by death" (v. 20).

It is likely that this was similar to the prayer the Jerusalem Christians prayed for Peter. They knew Herod's evil mind. They also knew that God never promised protection from the sword.

Peter's Restful Night (Acts 12:6)

Evidence shows that God answered the prayers of the church. The night before Peter was to be brought to trial, he was sound asleep—even though he was chained to two guards.

Identify with Peter for a moment. You know you are to face trial the next day. You know Herod's ruthless character and how much his ego has been affected by the Jews who want you dead. You know the Apostle James has already been tried and killed. And you know that sooner or later you'll suffer martyrdom because of what Jesus prophesied. *Yet* you're sound asleep!

Tranquility at a moment like that is supernatural. The natural disposition of a man on death row is anything but peaceful. This illustrates what God can do to our hearts when we commit our difficulties to Him in prayer. "Do not be anxious about anything, but in everything, by prayer and petition, with thanksgiving present your requests to God. And the *peace of God,* which transcends all understanding, will guard your hearts and your minds in Christ Jesus" (Phil. 4:6-7).

Surely, this must be the explanation for Peter's restful night at this rather dreadful time in his life. Surely this is a clue to the prayer content of those who had met to intercede for their beloved friend and leader.

Peter's Release (Acts 12:7-11)

What transpired that night shows that Peter did not expect to be set free—at least not that night. When the angel awakened him, when the chains fell from his wrists, when he walked by the first set of guards and then the second, and when he actually walked through the iron gate to the city which opened by itself allowing him to walk through—he still thought he was dreaming. What was happening could not be—even though he'd had a similar experience once before. It appears Peter could not accept the possibility it could happen twice—especially since James had not been released.

When it really dawned on Peter that he was free, he exclaimed, "Now I know without a doubt that the Lord sent His angel and rescued me from Herod's clutches and from everything the Jewish people were anticipating" (12:11).

What were the Jewish people anticipating? There is only one logical answer. Death by the sword—just as it had happened to James. This also explains why the Christians who had gathered to pray would not initially believe what they were about to see and learn. They too expected death for Peter.

Peter's Surprise Appearance (Acts 12:12-17)

The end of this tense and dramatic story is quite humorous. Peter immediately went to John Mark's home where the church had gathered to pray, evidence he knew about this prayer meeting. When he knocked at the outer entrance, a servant girl named Rhoda appeared. When she recognized Peter's voice, she was so excited she forgot to let him in. She ran back and exclaimed, "Peter is at the door!"

The people responded, "You're out of your mind!" When she kept insisting it was Peter, they could only conclude, "It must be his angel" (12:15). In their minds, he was already dead—again evidence that their prayers were not directed at his release.

When they finally heard from Peter's own lips what had happened "they were astonished" (v. 16). God had gone far beyond anything they'd asked for or thought possible. He had not only given Peter a sense of peace and tranquility to face what seemed certain death, but He had—at the very last minute—delivered Peter from Herod's evil plan.

Epilogue

Since Herod plays such a prominent role in this story, we cannot conclude this chapter without observing what happened to him. When he discovered Peter had escaped, he was livid with anger. No doubt humiliated and embarrassed, he tried to direct the public's critical eye away from himself by having the guards executed. Rather than recognizing God's supernatural work in the event and turning to God, he only became entrenched in his own egomania.

Luke gives us an even greater insight into what motivated this man. For some reason, Herod had been disputing with the people of Tyre and Sidon—another group of his subjects. These people knew Herod would have the final word and they feared he would retaliate by cutting off their food supply. But they also knew he was a terribly proud and ego-driven monarch. So they conspired to feed his ego, thus hoping to win his favor.

While Herod was delivering a public address, they cried out, "This is the voice of a god, not a man" (Acts 12:22). Herod, no doubt, responded with great arrogance, accepting the tribute as a statement of truth. At that moment, God's judgment fell on Herod. "Immediately, because Herod did not give praise to God, an angel of the Lord struck him down, and he was eaten by worms and died" (v. 23).

How ironic! Peter, who was to die by Herod's sword, was released by "an angel of the Lord." And Herod, who was to ask for Peter's death, was struck down by "an angel of the Lord."

Some Questions
Would God have released Peter if the church had not been praying?

We really don't know, but He probably would have. There are things we know we do not receive because we do not ask (James 4:2). There are things we don't receive because "we ask with wrong motives" (v. 3). But sometimes God does things far beyond our expectations—even when we don't ask.

The fact is the church was praying. God no doubt answered their prayers. God wants us to pray about everything. There is little value in this kind of hypothetical question. It only results in theological speculation that is meaningless, irrelevant, and confusing.

Would it have been proper for the Christians to pray specifically for Peter's release?

The answer is an unequivocal yes, *if* they had done so asking that God's will be done. They had no evidence that God was going to release Peter. In fact, all evidence pointed the other way. But God specializes in surprises. He delights in giving us things we don't even ask for, especially when we pray unselfishly and for His glory.

An Old Testament Illustration (1 Kings 3:4-15)

When Solomon became King of Israel, God appeared to him in a dream and said, "Ask for whatever you want Me to give you" (1 Kings 3:5).

How would the average person respond to this kind of communication from the Lord? More specifically, how would a king respond? More than likely he would ask for a long and productive life . . . or for wealth . . . or for protection from his enemies.

But Solomon asked for none of these. Rather, he asked for discernment to govern the Children of Israel and for wisdom to discern between right and wrong. He admitted his fear of failure as a king and acknowledged his need for supernatural guidance and help.

God was very pleased with Solomon's request. Consequently, He gave Solomon what he asked for and more. "I will do what you have asked," God responded. "I will give you a wise and discerning heart, so that there will never have been anyone like you nor will there ever be." The Lord continued, "I will give you what you *have not asked for*—both riches and honor—so that in your lifetime, you will have no equal among kings. And if you walk in My ways and obey My statutes and commands as David your father did, I will give you a long life" (3:12-14).

Is there a correlation between what God did for Peter and what He did for Solomon? Perhaps. God is pleased when we pray unselfishly. Though it certainly would not have been wrong for Peter and the church to pray for release, God is pleased when we think of His purposes first and entrust our total lives to Him, acknowledging that He knows best.

This illustration, which gives us insight into God's heart, shows us something about ourselves. As a parent, I respond very positively to my children when their attitude is one of trusting me to make wise decisions for them. In fact, there isn't anything I wouldn't do for them, if I could, and if I felt it was for their own best interest.

So it is with God. He is our heavenly Father and is on our team.

A Challenge

What about your prayer life? What about the prayer lives of those Christians with whom you worship? Maybe our focus is too much on ourselves—our personal comfort, deliverance from problems. Perhaps we should start praying for others—for their comfort and deliverance. Perhaps we should pray that whatever happens to us, we will—as Paul prayed—glorify God and never be ashamed of Him. Perhaps then God will surprise us.

But if He doesn't, we must trust Him for He knows what is best for His own honor and glory. Can we pray for ourselves and others—that He will be glorified—whether "by life or by death"?

During the 1930s when the Communists took over China, a young missionary couple was taken into custody. They were both killed because of their Christian faith. Their names were John and Betty Stam.

News of their martyrdom reached Dr. Will Houghton, then president of Moody Bible Institute, the school they attended for their training. Deeply moved by their deaths, he wrote the words to the following song, *By Life or By Death*. This song captures the attitude of men like Peter and Paul and other Christians who have faced severe persecution. The last stanza is a prayer. Will you make it your own?

So this is life, this world with all its pleasures,
Struggles and tears, a smile, a frown, a sigh,
Friendship so true, and love of kin and neighbor,
Sometimes 'tis hard to live—always, to die!
The world moves on, so rapidly the living
The forms of those who disappear replace,

And each one dreams that he will be enduring—
How soon that one becomes the missing face!
In life or death—and life is surely flying,
The crib and coffin carved from the self-same tree.

In life or death—and death so soon is coming—
Escape I cannot, there's no place to flee—
But Thou, O God, hast life that is eternal;
That life is mine, a gift through Thy dear Son,
Help me to feel its flush and pulse supernal,
Assurance of the morn when life is done.

Help me to know the value of these hours,
Help me the folly of all waste to see;
Help me to trust the Christ who bore my sorrows,
And thus to yield for life or death to Thee.
In all my days be glorified, Lord Jesus,
In all my ways guide me with Thine own eye;
Just when and as Thou wilt, use me, Lord Jesus,
And then for me 'tis Christ, to live or die.

A Project

Reflect for a few minutes on the things God has given you, even
though you have not asked Him for them specifically. Make a
list, and then share them with your prayer group.

Fasting

To this point, we have followed the theme of prayer as it is unfolded by the Holy Spirit and exemplified by New Testament Christians in the Book of Acts. Interestingly, the next two major prayer events recorded by Luke include fasting.

This is the first time fasting is referred to in the Book of Acts. Of course, it cannot be proved that New Testament Christians did not fast until this point. I would speculate that they did, at least periodically. But it seems safe to conclude that since the Holy Spirit did not choose to record this function till Acts 13, it bears careful consideration and study. We'll see both events recorded in Acts 13 and 14 include similar dynamics.

The Commissioning of Paul and Barnabas
(Acts 13:1-3)

Next to the church in Jerusalem, more is said about the church in Antioch than any other church in the Book of Acts. From a historian's point of view, this is logical for the church in Jerusalem was the *first* church. It was here in this great center of Judaism that the Christian movement was born. It was here that law and grace merged into one unified system of belief and doctrine.

Antioch, on the other hand, represents the beginning of the

second phase in the development of the church. Here the first intensified effort of preaching the Gospel to the Gentiles took place, launching another new phenomenon. The church in Jerusalem was the first body of Christian Jews. But the church in Antioch was seemingly the first major body of believers composed of Christians who were *both* Jews and Gentiles. And it was in Antioch that the missionary movement to the rest of the world was born.

Paul and Barnabas were the first Christians sent out by a church to plant other churches among the Gentiles. We have an account of that event in Acts 13:1-3. A group of men identified as "prophets and teachers" were meeting together (v. 1). "While they were worshiping the Lord and *fasting,* the Holy Spirit said, 'Set apart for Me Barnabas and Saul for the work to which I have called them' " (v. 2). That *work* was to carry the Gospel to the world beyond the confines of Jerusalem, Judea, and Samaria—out to the uttermost parts of the earth (1:8).

The other men recognized immediately God's call in the lives of Paul and Barnabas. "So after they had *fasted* and *prayed,* they placed their hands on them and sent them off" (v. 3).

In this unique setting involving prayer and fasting, God made His will clear regarding which men should be sent on this first missionary journey. Then before the other men commissioned Paul and Barnabas to this work, they spent time in *prayer* and *fasting.*

The Commissioning of Elders (Acts 14:21-23)

When Paul and Barnabas set out on this first missionary journey, they traveled to a number of strategic cities. In most cities they won converts to Christ and established churches.

There came a time, however, when they felt it was necessary to return to a number of cities to strengthen and encourage these new believers. In many instances they left these new Christians under very difficult circumstances involving persecution. Paul and Barnabas were deeply concerned that these churches grow and develop and not be thwarted and discouraged by those who resisted the Gospel.

One reason for returning to these cities was to appoint elders—spiritual leaders who could pastor and teach these people. It is also noteworthy that Paul and Barnabas included in this process a time of *prayer* and *fasting*. "Paul and Barnabas appointed elders for them in each church and, with *prayer and fasting,* committed them to the Lord in whom they put their trust" (14:23).

There is no evidence that the Holy Spirit gave specific directions as to whom to appoint in these churches as He had done when He called Paul and Barnabas. This is understandable because there is no evidence that God continued on a regular basis to use direct revelation as a means to make His will clear when early church leaders were appointed. In fact, Paul appears to be teaching that eldership is a position that any man may desire (1 Tim. 3:1). But it does seem significant that even though direct revelation was involved in one situation, and "good judgment based upon what God has already revealed regarding godliness" in another, yet in both instances, those making the appointments engaged in *prayer and fasting.*

Before thinking specifically about the way these two passages in Acts relate to us, it's important to understand more of what the Bible teaches about fasting and how it relates to prayer.

Three Kinds of Biblical Fasts

The first and most common kind of fast referred to in Scripture was the *normal* fast. It consisted of abstaining from food, but not from water. It usually lasted one day, though Christ evidently engaged in this kind of fast for 40 days.

The second kind of fast, which involved abstaining from both food and water, was the *absolute* fast. It is rarely mentioned in Scripture, and when it is, it represented some very unique circumstances. For example, Moses engaged in this kind of fast for 40 days and nights in the presence of the Lord on Mount Sinai (Ex. 34:28). This was definitely a miracle, for it is dangerous to go without water for even one day.

The third kind of fast was a *partial* fast. Participants restricted their normal intake of food as well as refrained from certain kinds of food. Daniel engaged in this kind of fast for three weeks (Dan. 10:2).

Five Biblical Guidelines

1. Fasting is never commanded in Scripture. There is no question but that prayer is to be a regular spiritual exercise for Christians. Again and again we are exhorted to pray. But this is not true of fasting. Even in the Old Testament, fasting seems to have been a purely voluntary act—something God's children chose to do. Jesus Himself never commanded His followers to fast, though He allowed freedom to do so, particularly after He returned to heaven (Matt. 9:14-15).

Unfortunately, throughout church history fasting became obligatory and ritualistic. When Jesus walked the earth, the Pharisees fasted regularly on the second and fifth day of every week (Monday and Thursday), assuming the act itself would impress God (Luke 18:12).

Eventually the same thing happened in the church. Following the pattern established by the Pharisees, Christian leaders appointed Wednesday and especially Friday as days for partial fasting. They abstained from eating meat to commemorate the Crucifixion of Jesus.

Next, certain periods for fasting were established. The period of fasting before Easter came to be known as Lent. Initially, the instructions for fasting were very specific, allowing only 1 meal a day and no meat for 40 days. The 40-day period was no doubt based on the fact that both Moses and Jesus fasted for 40 days.

By the 6th century, fasting became an obligation in the established church. Anyone who did not fast was disciplined. By the 8th century, fasting was considered a means to gain merit with God. Those who did not participate were excommunicated from the church.

Unfortunately, Christians took what God wanted to be a *freedom* and made it a *requirement.* In doing so, fasting lost its significance and true meaning. This leads us to a second biblical guideline.

2. When we fast, we should do so with proper motives. As we've already seen in our study on prayer, God is concerned about our motives. James made this point very clear. He wrote, "When you ask, you do not receive because you ask with wrong motives" (James 4:3). Jesus was even more specific when He taught about fasting. One day He said to the multitudes who came to hear Him on a mountainside:

> When you fast, do not look somber as the hypocrites do, for they disfigure their faces to show men they are fasting. I tell you the truth, they have received their reward in full. But when you fast, put oil on your head and wash your face, so that it will not be obvious to men that you are fasting, but only to your Father, who is unseen; and your Father, who sees what is done in secret, will reward you (Matt. 6:16-18).

Jesus was not teaching that it is wrong for other Christians to know that we are fasting, just as He was *not* teaching that other Christians should not know when we are praying or when we are giving. Jesus had also stated that we should not pray in public but in secret (Matt. 6:5-6), and that when we give we should give in secret (vv. 2-4). We miss His point completely when we do not understand the context. The Pharisees' motives for giving, praying, and fasting were all wrong. They were showing off. Thus Jesus introduced these subjects by saying, "Be careful not to do your acts of righteousness before men, *to be seen by them.* If you do, you will have no reward from your Father in heaven" (v. 1).

We miss what Christ was teaching if we focus on secrecy rather than motives. It *is* possible for Christians to give, fast, and pray publicly with right motives. Christians who do these things with right motives are models of godliness and righteousness—and all of us need those models.

However, if we do these things only to glorify ourselves, then we'd better develop an approach that puts our motives to the test. This was what Jesus was doing. He knew that emphasizing secrecy with the hypocritical Pharisees would totally unveil their pride, arrogance, and false motives. He put them in an awkward position; every reason they had for "performing their acts of righteousness" would be eliminated—except glorifying God. Since they were *only glorifying themselves,* they would have no reason to do any of these things. On occasions, it would probably be good for all of us as Christians to ask ourselves: *Would I be as faithful in doing what I do for Jesus Christ if others were not watching?*

3. Fasting appears to be more appropriate and necessary in crisis situations. Fasting during periods of extreme difficulty is biblically illustrated, especially in the Old Testament. Nehemiah's experience stands out as a prime example. While serving as cup bearer to King Artaxerxes, Nehemiah received word from Jerusalem that his fellow Jews were "in great trouble and disgrace" because the walls of Jerusalem had been "broken down" and the gates "burned with fire" (Neh. 1:1-3). Nehemiah was so disturbed about the situation that he "sat down and wept" and for a number of days, he "mourned and fasted and prayed before the God of heaven" (v. 4).

Because Nehemiah's motives for praying and fasting were right, the Lord honored his spirit of humility and selflessness. In this crisis, God answered Nehemiah's prayer in a marvelous way.

But we have another example where one of God's choicest servants prayed and fasted and the Lord *did not* answer. David, King of Israel, sinned terribly by committing adultery with Bathsheba and murdering her husband.

By Old Testament Law, David should have died for his sin. However, God had mercy because of David's deep and sincere repentance. Through the Prophet Nathan, God made it clear that the child born from David's illegitimate union would die instead (2 Sam. 12:14).

David did not initially accept this verdict. He "pleaded with God for the child. He *fasted* and went into his house and spent the nights lying on the ground" (v. 16). Though the elders in his household tried to get him to arise and eat, David steadfastly refused.

Seven days later, the child died. When David got the bad news, he immediately got up, stopped weeping, bathed, worshiped God in the temple, and then ate. His servants were confused by this radical change in his behavior. David explained, "While the child was still alive, I fasted and wept. I thought, 'Who knows? The Lord may be gracious to me and let the child live.' But now that he is dead, why should I fast? Can I bring him back again? I will go to him, but he will not return to me" (vv. 22-23).

Were David's motives proper? It appears they were at that point in his life. However, God did not honor David's request. David knew that he, himself, deserved to die. God had already shown mercy, and in this deep grief, David felt free to ask God for *more* mercy—even though he did not deserve it. He knew the Lord often responds to prayer and fasting in difficult circumstances.

It's important to underscore however that David knew that God might not answer because of the seriousness of the sin he had committed before all Israel and also before the enemy of God's people (v. 14). He showed no anger or bitterness toward the Lord when his prayer was not answered. This indeed is one reason why David was called a man after God's own heart (Acts 13:22). In spite of David's many weaknesses, he had a soft and tender spirit toward God.

What about Christians today? We can learn valuable lessons from these Old Testament illustrations. God *does* respond to sincere prayer in crisis situations. *Fasting* is one way that we can demonstrate to the Lord our sincerity, our humility, and our willingness to forgo human desires in order to seek His help and His will. This leads us to another biblical guideline.

4. *God does not honor "fasting" per se, but what this action represents in our own lives.* God responds to fasting combined with prayer because it shows Him our willingness to forgo meeting our personal needs in order to spend time with Him. It appears that this is also true of sexual abstinence. Paul spoke to this issue in his letter to the Corinthians. Evidently these people, because of their pagan religious backgrounds in the way

sexual relationships were abused, believed that sexual abstinence would somehow increase their spirituality or gain them
special favor with God. Paul made it clear that marital partners
have a responsibility to each other. "Do not deprive each other
except by mutual consent and for a time, so that you may
devote yourselves to prayer" (1 Cor. 7:5).

God does not honor abstaining from sexual relationships in
marriage per se any more than He honors abstaining from food.
Rather, He honors the fact that we are willing to forgo personal
needs for a period of time in order to spend that time in prayer.
Practically speaking, this means that the time we would be
spending meeting our own needs should be spent in fellowship
with God.

5. *The Book of Acts models for us that prayer and fasting
is a means whereby a body of believers may seek God's will in
the appointment of church leaders.* Compared with the Old
Testament, there is little recorded in the New Testament on
fasting. The letters to the New Testament churches include
many instructions and exhortations regarding both corporate
and personal prayer. But there are no instructions or exhortations to fast. This only substantiates the fact that we have
freedom to fast, but we must not allow fasting to become an
obligation or even an expectation in the church.

The two illustrations in the Book of Acts involving Paul and
Barnabas speak clearly to the church. If this is true, what is God
saying to us? Why is this the first time fasting is mentioned in
the Book of Acts and why is it combined with prayer? Is it
possible that leadership appointments in the church—whether
it be those who are commissioned to start new churches or those
who are appointed to serve in already established churches—
should be taken more seriously than many of us have in the past
considered?

It is my opinion that God is saying this very thing. Prayer combined with fasting seems to be the process that God
uses to make His will clear in the hearts of those who are appointing leaders as well as in the hearts of those who are to be
appointed.

Not that the Holy Spirit will speak directly as He did in Antioch! But, He can "speak" through a body of Christians who seriously seek His will in prayer and fasting. This is especially true when we consider the will of God which has already been revealed, such as the qualities by which we should select leaders (see 1 Tim. 3:1-13; Titus 1:5-9).

A Challenge
How should 20th-century Christians respond to the biblical truth in this chapter?

First, if we practice fasting as a spiritual exercise, we must not be judgmental of others who do not. If we are, we may be in danger of violating the second biblical guideline; that is, our motives may be wrong.

Second, we should not be hesitant to fast when we face crisis situations—even crises that are of our own making. Certainly we can learn this from David's experience.

Third, we should make sure that time spent in fasting is used to pray and commune with God. Most of us spend several hours each day eating. Periodic fasting allows us to spend that time in fellowship with God.

Fourth, we should encourage our church leaders to consider the combination of prayer and fasting as a valid process for determining God's will in selecting and appointing church leaders. This can be done by the present leadership in a church as they seek to appoint new or additional leaders. It can be done by a select group in the church. Or it can be done by the whole church. But it must never become ritualistic or obligatory. Those who do not choose to participate should never be condemned.

A Final Note
Some who advocate fasting say that if it is done properly, it contributes not only to our spiritual well-being but to our mental and physical health. In his book, *How to Keep Healthy and Happy by Fasting* (Harvest House), Salem Kirban lists these physical and mental benefits of fasting:

- It cleans out the body.
- It gives the digestive system a rest.

- It sharpens our mental processes.
- It helps us control our weight.

These are valid benefits. However, the Bible nowhere suggests that these are the benefits of fasting. This does not mean, of course, that they are not true.

On the other hand, some people should never fast, particularly beyond 24 hours. Any person experiencing physical problems should not fast without consulting a physician. This is the exception not the rule, for most of us are healthy and would probably improve our health by periodic, short-term fasting. If our motives are right, and if we use the time to pray, we'll also benefit spiritually—the primary reason for biblical fasting.

> *Dear Father, I pray that I'll be faithful in prayer itself. Guide me in considering the truth in this chapter. Help me not to be so occupied with my own physical needs that I am not willing to temporarily forgo meeting those needs to spend time with You. I pray that my church leaders may consider emulating Paul and Barnabas as they appoint spiritual leaders.*

A Project

If you feel comfortable doing so and if there are no medical reasons why you shouldn't, consider a one-day normal fast, drinking only water or juice. Use the time you would ordinarily spend eating, reading your Bible and praying. Concentrate on some special area in your life you wish to bring more into conformity with God's will.

10

Paul's Personal Petitions

From this point forward in the Book of Acts the theme of prayer focuses primarily on the Apostle Paul. This is logical because Luke outlines the missionary journeys, Paul's final trip back to Jerusalem and then to Rome, where the biblical account ends with his imprisonment. Tradition informs us that Paul was martyred in Rome at the hands of Nero.

Paul believed in prayer. It was a consistent part of his personal and public life. When he arrived in Philippi on his second missionary journey, he immediately went to the "place of prayer" (Acts 16:13). It seems clear from Luke's account that he often spent time there (v. 16).

Two other examples are recorded in conjunction with Paul's trip to Jerusalem. While on the way, he stopped at Miletus and asked the elders at Ephesus to meet him there. After sharing his concern for them and the church, "he knelt down with all of them and prayed" (20:36).

What a beautiful scene this must have been as these men wept aloud and "embraced [Paul] and kissed him" (v. 37). They were particularly grieved because they knew that Paul was headed for serious trouble and that they would probably never see him again. As far as we know, they didn't. Prayer became particularly meaningful at that moment in their lives.

There was another beautiful "prayer scene" when Paul arrived by ship in Tyre. While the cargo was being unloaded, Paul spent seven days ministering to the Christians in that city. On the day he left, whole families escorted him to the ship. There on the beach they all knelt together and prayed—men, women, and children (21:5).

Though these examples in the Book of Acts tell us a great deal about Paul's view of prayer, the letters he wrote to the churches tell us far more. In this chapter we want to look at three specific prayers, focusing primarily on his prayer for the Christians at Ephesus.

Paul's Prayer for the Ephesians

Actually two of Paul's prayers are recorded in the Book of Ephesians. However, they can really be viewed as one prayer since the second is an extension of the first. This becomes very clear when they are put together, as illustrated in the grammatical layout in Figure 4.

For this reason . . .

Paul actually used this concept three times in the first three chapters of Ephesians to give continuity to his thoughts (Eph. 1:15; 3:1, 14). The reason or cause he is referring to is the Ephesians' spiritual growth. He was pleased and excited about their progress in faith and love. He was also encouraged that God had allowed him to be a part of their conversion and spiritual growth.

A careful look at the flow of Paul's thoughts shows that his first prayer is connected to the second prayer and interrupted by a detailed explanation of God's power and grace in their lives (1:19—2:22), and in his own life (3:1-13). Paul then continues his prayer in Ephesians 3:14. The phrase *for this reason* demonstrates that continuity, particularly in our English translations.

I have not stopped . . . I keep on asking . . .

Paul's commitment to persistence in prayer is illustrated with these two statements. For him, prayer was indeed a *steadfast*

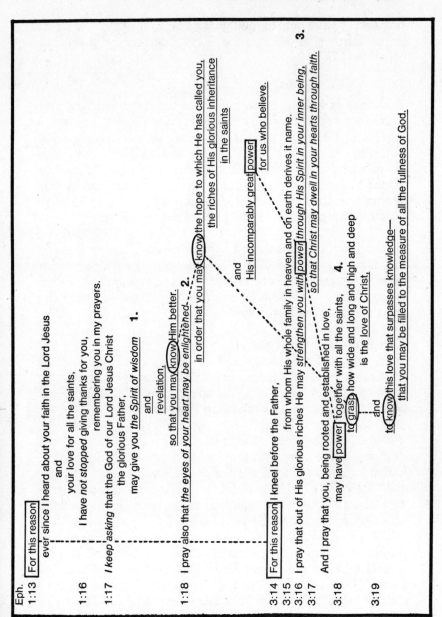

Figure 4

process. "I have not stopped giving thanks for you," he wrote (1:16). Further, he *kept asking* God for certain things on their behalf (v. 17).

That you may know . . .
The ideas of knowing, grasping, and understanding are very prominent in this prayer. From Paul's words and the overall context of his prayer, we see that he was not talking about superficial knowledge, but "full knowledge." Obviously, the Ephesians already *knew* God in Christ. This is why Paul was writing to them and praying for them. But beyond that, he was praying that they might come to know, understand, and experience *much more* about their great calling in Christ.

His incomparably great power . . .
The word *power* is another key concept in Paul's prayer for these believers. It is very important to understand what Paul meant, which we'll look at more in depth as we study the specific content of this prayer.

The Specific Content
In this prayer Paul mentioned four *requests* and four *reasons* for these requests. He then culminates his prayer in the opening verse of chapter 4 by stating the specific *results* that will occur when this prayer is answered (see Figure 5).

The Spirit of wisdom and revelation
Paul was not praying that they would *receive* the Holy Spirit. Earlier he acknowledged that they had already been "marked" and "sealed" by the Holy Spirit (1:13). Rather, Paul was praying that they would have "spiritual wisdom and understanding" (Col. 1:9) and "depth of insight" (Phil. 1:9).

The Holy Spirit, of course, is the ultimate Source of this wisdom and knowledge. That is why Jesus referred to Him several times in the Upper Room discourse as the "Spirit of Truth" (John 14:17; 15:26; 16:13) when He told the apostles that He would send them "another Counselor" (14:16).

SPECIFIC REQUESTS   **SPECIFIC REASONS**

1. Give you the Spirit of wisdom
   and revelation ⟶ so that you may know Him better
   (Eph. 1:17).

2. The eyes of your heart may
   be enlightened ⟶ in order that you may know the hope
   to which He has called you,
   a. the riches of His glorious
      inheritance in the saints,
   b. His incomparably great power
      for us who believe (1:18-19).

3. Strengthen you with power
   through His Spirit in your
   inner being ⟶ so that Christ may dwell in your
   hearts through faith (3:16).

4. Power . . . to grasp . . . the love
   of Christ, and to know this love
   that surpasses knowledge ⟶ that you may be filled to the
   measure of all the fullness of God
   (3:18-19).

SPECIFIC RESULT
To live a life worthy of the calling you have received (4:1).

Figure 5

Jesus also specified clearly what the Holy Spirit's primary ministry would be:

- Teach you all things (14:26).
- Remind you of everything I've said to you (v. 26).
- Testify about Me (15:26).
- Convict the world of guilt in regard to sin and righteousness and judgment (16:8).
- Guide you into all truth (16:13).
- Tell you what is yet to come (16:13).

In the early days of the church, the Holy Spirit spoke directly through the apostles as He promised. Fortunately, God's plan for communication with mankind involved the New Testament which was written primarily by the apostles and inspired by the Holy Spirit (2 Tim. 3:16-17). Today we have access to the totality of God's "wisdom and revelation" in the Scriptures. In that sense we have a unique advantage over New Testament Christians who had limited access to God's truth. Through the written Word of God we can discover who God truly is and what He's done for us in Jesus Christ. This leads us to the specific *reason* Paul prayed that the Ephesians would have "the Spirit of wisdom and revelation" (Eph. 1:17).

So that you may know Him better

As we study the Scriptures, we can learn *about* God. But that knowledge should be more than theological. It should also be experiential.

We can illustrate this in a limited sense by our relationships with people. When I first met my wife Elaine, I began to learn things about her. It didn't take long for me to see that she was attractive. Eventually, I discovered that she was very intelligent. I learned a lot about her early life—that she grew up on a farm in Minnesota, that she had three older sisters, that her father was a full-blooded Swede and her mother a full-blooded German. As I spent time with her, I began to know her better. Over the last number of years since we've been married (we passed the 25-year mark in 1981), I have *really* come to know her better. Of course, this has been a reciprocal process. In fact,

I'm sure there are things my wife has learned about me she wishes were not true.

Since both of us are created in God's image, there is still a lot more to learn about each other. Our knowledge is no longer just cognitive and intellectual like it was in the early days of our relationship. It is now intensely affective and experiential.

Thus Paul prays that the Ephesian Christians might come to know *God* better. The primary source of that knowledge is God's Word, revealed by the Holy Spirit.

The eyes of your heart may be enlightened

The Holy Spirit not only inspired the authors of Scripture to write the truth, but He desires to help all Christians *understand* the truth He has revealed. One primary way God enlightens us is through prayer. This is why Paul prayed for the Ephesians. We too should pray regularly that the Holy Spirit will open our hearts and minds to understand God's Word, not only intellectually but experientially.

Paul then explained why Christians need enlighened hearts.

In order that you may know the hope
to which He has called you

The Ephesians were strong in *faith* and *love* (1:15), but uncertain in their *hope*. This was probably true in a special way among the Gentile converts. Paul reassured them that even though they were not Jews and were initially "excluded from citizenship in Israel and foreigners to the covenants of the promise" and *"without hope"* (2:12), this was no longer true. The "dividing wall" between Jews and Gentiles had been removed by Jesus Christ who "made the two one" (v. 14). Thus Paul later reminded them they "were called to *one hope*" and they were to live in the light of that oneness and unity (4:4).

Paul, in this prayer, elaborates on that hope. It involves the fact that we are Christ's inheritance, given to Him by the Father (1:18). Our hope and security are not based on our ability or faithfulness, but on God's eternal power—the same power that raised Jesus Christ from the dead (v. 20). In God's sight we are already raised up with Christ and seated with Him in "heavenly realms" (2:6). Knowing this not only with our heads but with our hearts gives us inner strength.

Strengthen you with power through His Spirit in your inner being

Here Paul was referring both to external power and internal power. There's the power of God "which He exerted in Christ when He raised Him from the dead and seated Him at His right hand in heavenly realms" (1:20). Paul informed the Ephesians that it was the same power that raised them up with Christ and seated them with Him (2:6). In other words, it took the same power to save us from our sins as it did to raise Jesus Christ from the dead.

Paul also referred to *internal* power and strength that is released within our hearts and inner beings. This power is rooted in two sources. First, this power is released when we truly *know, understand, and comprehend* how secure our position is in Christ. This power is based on knowledge and truth. In this sense, the power is psychological strength that comes from being *sure* of our position in Christ.

The second source of internal power relates directly to God's indwelling Spirit. However, it is clear from Paul's prayer that this power is intrinsically related to knowledge and truth. The power of God's Spirit is released in our lives through our experiential interaction with both the written Word (Scripture) and the Living Word (Jesus Christ).

So that Christ may dwell in your hearts through faith

Jesus Christ was no longer visible when Paul wrote to the Ephesians. Nevertheless, He was alive and through His Spirit He was living within their hearts.

To accept this reality, however, involves faith. To be vital, faith must be based on facts, even though these facts reflect invisible realities. The author of the Book of Hebrews stated that "faith is being sure of what we hope for and certain of what we do not see" (Heb. 11:1).

The apostles and many other New Testament Christians saw Christ. They walked with Him, touched Him, and lived with Him. They saw Him die, and more important, they saw the undeniable evidence that He was indeed raised from the dead. They heard Him speak of His return and saw Him return to heaven.

Paul too saw Christ, but miraculously so. This was a privilege afforded very few people after the Lord Jesus returned to heaven. The Ephesians could only respond to what they *heard* about Christ. True, in the early days of the church, God bore witness to the message of Christ and salvation "by signs, wonders, and various miracles, and gifts of the Holy Spirit" (Heb. 2:4). The Ephesians saw many of these "extraordinary miracles" (Acts 19:11-12).

But the fact remains that Jesus was no longer visible. The temptation, particularly in the midst of persecution and difficulties, would be to grow weary and to waiver spiritually. Thus Paul prayed that the Ephesians would have inner strength through a knowledge of the Word of God and through the ministry of God's Spirit to keep on believing and trusting the living Christ. The result would be "endurance and patience, and joyfully giving thanks to the Father" (Col. 1:11-12).

Power ... to grasp ... the love of Christ

To understand and comprehend the extent of Christ's love is a supernatural process. It can only be accomplished by means of God's divine help and power. All the facts in the world cannot help us truly understand it all. In fact, Christ's love "surpasses knowledge."

The key to helping a Christian comprehend the extent of God's love is prayer. This is why Paul prayed specifically for the Ephesians—and for us—that Christians of all time might indeed "have power, together with *all the saints,* to grasp how wide and long and high and deep is the love of Christ and to know this love that surpasses knowledge" (3:18-19).

That you may be filled to the measure of all fullness of God
To be filled with God's fullness means, first and foremost, being filled "with the knowledge of God" and "His will" (Col. 1:10-11)—who He is, what He has done for us, and what He desires in our lives. Paul was not speaking of some ecstatic and super-charged experience. It is true that this kind of knowledge will touch not only our intellect, but also our emotions. However, God designed a process that should be ongoing, deepening with each passing day till Christ comes again. When this happens, our knowledge of "God's fullness" will affect our total being—including the way we live.

To live a life worthy of the calling you have received
In Ephesians 4:1 Paul stated what should result from all that he had prayed. We should live lives worthy of the Lord. In fact, he outlined in detail what this meant:
- We should "no longer live as the Gentiles do" (4:17).
- We should "live a life of love, just as Christ loved us" (5:2).
- We should "live as children of light" (v. 8).
- We should "be very careful how [we] live" (v. 15).

A true knowledge of God and His deep and great love for us will affect the way we live. In fact, if we don't become more sensitive to sin as we live our Christian lives, we are not growing in our knowledge of God and His will.

Corollary Prayers
Following are two prayers from Paul's letters to the Colossians and the Philippians. These prayers are in essence the same prayers he prayed for the Ephesians. The Colossian prayer is more succinctly stated, and Paul moves quickly to the specific results, actually including them in detail in this prayer (see Figure 6). The Philippian prayer is even more succinct, reflecting perhaps that the Philippian Christians were already significantly advanced in their spiritual growth (see Figure 7).

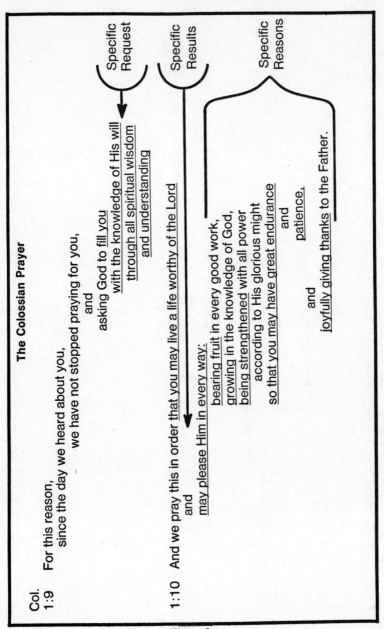

The Colossian Prayer

Col.
1:9   For this reason,
       since the day we heard about you,
       we have not stopped praying for you,
                and
                asking God to fill you
                     with the knowledge of His will
                          through all spiritual wisdom
                               and understanding

       Specific Request

1:10   And we pray this in order that you may live a life worthy of the Lord
                and
       may please Him in every way:
                bearing fruit in every good work,
                growing in the knowledge of God,
                being strengthened with all power
                     according to His glorious might
                     so that you may have great endurance
                                and
                                patience,
                                and
                joyfully giving thanks to the Father.

       Specific Results

       Specific Reasons

Figure 6

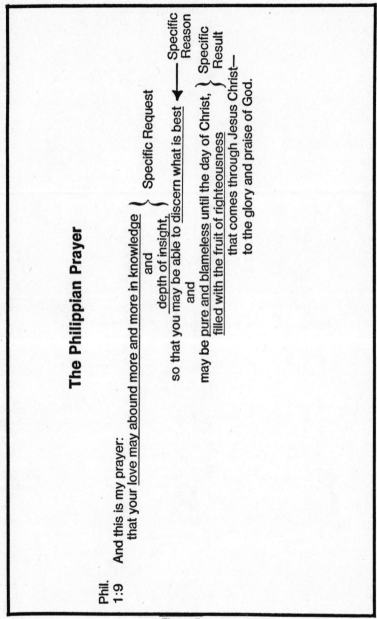

The Philippian Prayer

Phil.
1:9

And this is my prayer:
that your love may abound more and more in knowledge
and
depth of insight,
} Specific Request

so that you may be able to discern what is best ← Specific Reason
and
may be pure and blameless until the day of Christ,
filled with the fruit of righteousness
that comes through Jesus Christ—
to the glory and praise of God.
} Specific Result

Figure 7

Personalizing Paul's Prayers

Paul's personal prayers for New Testament Christians form a beautiful personal or corporate prayer for every 20th-century Christian. Many churches use the Lord's Prayer—which is indeed appropriate. However, the literal application of that prayer will no doubt be fulfilled some future day when Christ once again deals with His people in Israel.

Paul's personal prayers for the churches are directly applicable in *every respect* now. You may wish to use the following prayer periodically, both in your personal time with God as well as when your church gathers to worship the Lord.

Glorious Father, please grant me spiritual wisdom and understanding. Fill me with the knowledge of Your will so that I may know You better. May my heart be enlightened that I may know the hope to which You have called me; the hope that is based in Your grace and love that chose me in Christ Jesus before the creation of the world; the hope that is based on the same power that raised Jesus Christ from the dead and seated Him at Your right hand.

I pray that You'll strengthen me with Your power through Your Spirit in my inner being so that Christ may dwell in my heart through faith. May I have power to grasp how wide and long and high and deep Christ's love for me really is. May I know this love that surpasses knowledge so that I may be filled to the measure of the fullness of God.

All this I pray, Father, that I may live a life worthy of You and may please You in every way. As I grow in my knowledge of You, may I bear fruit in every good work. Grant that I may have endurance and patience and joyfully give thanks to You, Father, for my position in Christ.

*May my love abound more and more in knowledge
and depth of insight so that I can truly discern what
is best and that I may be pure and blameless till the
Day of Christ, filled with the fruit of righteousness
that comes through Your Son, Jesus Christ. All of this
I pray so that You may be praised and glorified, dear
Father.*

A Project

Use this prayer as a corporate prayer by changing all of the
personal pronouns to plural pronouns. You may suggest to your
pastor that this prayer be used in your church's worship service.
Or you may want to use it in your Sunday School class, Bible
study group, or fellowship group.

11

God's Peace

Paul not only exemplified prayer in his own life, but he also gave us some practical instructions regarding this divine process. "Do not be anxious about anything, but in everything, by prayer and petition, with thanksgiving, present your requests to God. And the peace of God which transcends all understanding, will guard your hearts and your minds in Christ Jesus" (Phil. 4:6-7).

In this passage Paul treated a basic problem that *all* Christians face at times—the problem of anxiety. However, he presented a solution—prayer—and then stated the ultimate result of this process—the peace of God.

What kinds of problems did Paul have in mind? Is prayer really the means by which we can overcome anxiety? And what did Paul mean by the "peace of God"?

The Basic Problem—Anxiety
Paul's initial statement is succinct and clear—"Do not be anxious about anything" (Phil. 4:6).

The basic word in the *Greek New Testament* which is translated *anxious* means to be "troubled" or "worried." It also refers to being "pulled" or "drawn in different directions"—the opposite of having a sense of inner harmony and peace.

Paul's statement, though concise, is also comprehensive. We

113

are not to be "anxious about *anything.*" There's *nothing* that comes into a Christian's experience causing worry or anxiety that is outside of God's concern for His children. He's interested in every detail of our lives.

Though many of life's details and factors cause anxiety, certain areas are common sources of worry. These areas are also outlined and illustrated in Scripture. Let's look at three.

Our Material Needs (Matt. 6:25-34)
Jesus spoke about this problem in what has come to be called His Sermon on the Mount. In one section of His sermon, Jesus used the same basic word that Paul used in his letter to the Philippians. However, in the *New International Version,* the word is translated *worry* rather than *anxious.*

Note also that Jesus used this word five times:
- Therefore, I tell you do not *worry* about your life (Matt. 6:25).
- Who of you by *worrying* can add a single hour to his life? (v. 27)
- Why do you *worry* about clothes? (v. 28)
- So do not *worry,* saying "What shall we eat?" or "What shall we drink?" or "What shall we wear?" (v. 31).
- Therefore do not worry about tomorrow, for tomorrow will *worry* about itself (v. 34).

Obviously, Jesus was attempting to get a very important point across. Five times in this passage He told His listeners not to *worry* about the things they need on this earth.

Christ's illustrations in this passage are also very graphic, even in our culture. While He was sitting on the mountainside, He probably gestured to the birds that were flying overhead and also to the lilies growing on the hills. Thus, He said:

Look at the *birds* of the air; they do not sow or reap or store away in barns, and yet your heavenly Father feeds them. Are *you* not much more valuable than they? (Matt. 6:26)

See how the *lilies* of the field grow. They do not labor or spin. Yet I tell you that not even Solomon in all his splendor was dressed like one of these. If that is how God clothes the grass of the field, which is here today and tomorrow is thrown into the fire, will He not much more clothe *you*, O you of little faith? (vv. 28-30)

Jesus summarized this rather powerful section of His Sermon on the Mount with a succinct statement. "But seek *first* His kingdom and His righteousness, and all these things will be given to you as well" (v. 33).

What Is Jesus Saying to Us?

The Sermon on the Mount contains a general body of truth that is supra-cultural. There were unique ways in which this message applied to Jews living in the Roman Empire in Jesus' day. Many believe there are unique ways in which it will be applied in some future day. But some principles emerge from this passage that should be applied to Christians in any period of history. One principle is that we must not allow our material needs to dominate our emotions and keep us constantly worried.

Jesus was *not* teaching that Christians should be irresponsible in these matters. In fact, the work ethic is prominent in Scripture. Paul, more than any other New Testament personality, both modeled and taught that ethic. He wrote to the Thessalonians, "If a man will not work, he shall not eat." Making the point even clearer, he continued, "We hear that some among you are idle. They are not busy; they are busybodies. Such people we command and urge in the Lord Jesus Christ, to settle down and earn the bread they eat" (2 Thes. 3:10-12).

Christians must be responsible people. But we must not allow our material needs to dominate our lives. We must put *first things first*. This is what Jesus meant when He said, "Seek first His kingdom and His righteousness." But He also recognized that we need material things, and thus He said—when we put God first in our lives "all these things will be given to [us] as well."

Our Daily Responsibilities (Luke 10:38-41)

This cause for anxiety was illustrated in a practical way when Jesus was visiting His close friends, Mary and Martha. While sitting in their home, Jesus began to teach. Mary immediately sat at His feet to listen.

Martha, on the other hand, got busy in the "kitchen." The more she worked making preparations, the more frustrated she got, and the more irritated she got at Mary. Finally, when she couldn't emotionally handle the situation any longer, Martha blurted out, "Lord, don't You care that my sister has left me to do the work by myself? Tell her to help me!" (Luke 10:40) Jesus' response was soft and beautiful. "Martha, Martha, . . . you are *worried* [anxious] and upset about many things, but only one thing is needed. Mary has chosen what is better, and it will not be taken away from her" (vv. 41-42).

Evidently, this was not an isolated experience in Martha's life. She had been "upset about *many things.*" The implication is that this was only one instance when she had been distracted, frustrated, and worried. Nervousness had become a part of her lifestyle. Today we would call this behavior obsessive-compulsive.

Jesus was not condoning irresponsibility. His words to Martha were not an excuse for a woman to have a messy house while she spent all her time going to church, Bible studies, and even prayer sessions. Nor was it an excuse for a woman to neglect preparing meals so she could spend time in personal devotions or listening to her favorite "television preacher." Rather, Jesus was emphasizing what He emphasized in the Sermon on the Mount—Christians should put first things first. We must not become so overwhelmed with daily responsibilities that we neglect the Lord. And we must not become so bogged down with activity—even spiritual activity—that we neglect "to sit at His feet" and listen to Him.

Relationships with Those Who Oppose Our Beliefs (1 Peter 4:12-16; 5:7)

This problem, more than any other, caused stress and anxiety for New Testament Christians. Often they were persecuted for their faith. In fact, this problem was foremost in Paul's mind when he encouraged the Philippians to pray about situations that caused anxiety. Earlier in the letter he had exhorted them to "stand firm in one spirit, contending as one man for the faith of the Gospel *without being frightened*" (Phil. 1:27-28). The Philippian Christians, like many others in the first-century world, faced unusual pressure and opposition from the pagan community.

The Apostle Peter, writing his letter to a number of churches scattered throughout the New Testament world (1 Peter 1:1-2), also wrote about the effect of persecution and trials on a Christian's physical and emotional well-being. "Dear friends, do not be surprised at the painful trial you are suffering as though something strange were happening to you" (4:12).

Peter did not deny that trials would create anxiety. There's no way to avoid an emotional response to problems. But Peter explained how believers should handle their problems. "Cast all your *anxiety* on Him because He cares for you" (5:7). This leads us to Paul's solution, for he specifically tells us *how* to cast our anxiety on the Lord.

The Primary Solution—Prayer

Paul's solution to anxiety is clear: "But in everything, by prayer and petition, with thanksgiving, present your requests to God" (Phil. 4:6).

With this statement Paul emphasized that nothing happens to a Christian that is outside of the sphere of God's personal love and concern. We have the right to pray about everything.

Note that Paul told the Philippians to pray *"with thanksgiving."* In essence he wrote the same thing to the Thessalonians. "Pray continually; *give thanks in all circumstances,* for this is God's will for you in Christ Jesus" (1 Thes. 5:17-18).

This concept has been woefully misinterpreted. Paul was not saying we have to thank God for pain and hurt and anxiety. Rather, in the midst of pain and hurt and anxiety—and even persecution—we are to thank God

- that He loves and cares for us;
- that we belong to Him;
- that He will not forsake us;
- that He will sustain us;
- that we have "an inheritance that can never perish" (1 Peter 1:4).

Perhaps most of all, we should thank God

- that He hears and answers prayer.

The Ultimate Result—Peace

"And the *peace of God* which transcends all understanding, will guard your hearts and your minds in Christ Jesus" (Phil. 4:7).

God never promises that we will be delivered from uncomfortable circumstances. If He did, He would have to remove us from this earth (so be careful how you pray). But He does promise to sustain us and give us peace in the midst of our difficulties. This is what Paul was saying to the Philippians.

The concept of peace is used frequently in Scripture. It is often used in an external sense to refer to harmony and unity among Christians. It is also used to refer to the harmony and unity that exists between a Christian and God because of what Christ has done through His death and resurrection, which is identified as "peace *with* God." Paul referred to this in his letter to the Romans. "Therefore, since we have been justified through faith, we have *peace with God* through our Lord Jesus Christ" (Rom. 5:1).

However, the Scriptures also use the word peace in an "internal" sense to refer to *inner* harmony and tranquility within a Christian's heart. There's no question that Paul, when writing to the Philippians, was referring to *inner* harmony and peace.

Someone has defined this inner peace as "the tranquil state of a soul assured of its salvation through Christ, and so fearing nothing from God and content with its earthly lot, of whatever sort that is" (Joseph Henry Thayer, *Greek-English Lexicon of the New Testament,* Zondervan, p. 182). Paul, in his letter to the Philippians, referred to this as the "peace *of* God." Through Christ we have "peace *with* God." This is *positional* truth. But in Christ, we can also have the "peace *of* God." This is a practical reality.

We cannot fully explain how this works. It transcends all understanding. For example, believers have met their deaths in martyrdom with inner peace that defies description or explanation. It is a supernatural experience.

Those of us who have never faced severe persecution cannot identify with the experience. Facing death—particularly at the hands of hostile people—is a fearful thought. But God's grace is endless. The greater our problem, the more grace God can provide. His reserves are infinite. Just believing that truth should give us inner strength to face whatever lies ahead.

My brother Wally's beautiful and talented wife Jana contracted incurable cancer in the prime of her life—age 40. All of us in the family were stunned and shocked.

Both Wally and Jana were dedicated Christians. They knew God could heal Jana, if it was His will, even though the doctors outlined the step-by-step process that this kind of cancer takes—leading rather quickly to death. But Wally and Jana also knew that God had not promised that He would always heal us.

The final days of Jana's life were an unbelievable testimony to all who knew her. Her private physician just shook his head in unbelief. God had given Jana unusual peace in the midst of a very difficult and painful experience. The same was true of Wally and their teenage children. God was answering prayer, for it is His will to give us *inner peace* in spite of our external circumstances.

This does not mean that there were no moments of emotional and physical pain, especially during Jana's final days. In fact, there were days that were almost unbearable. Nor did it stop all of us who knew them well from crying out in our anguish, "Why, O Lord?" But God gave inner peace in spite of our pain. *Prayer is the key that unlocks God's divine resources.*

The songwriter captures it well:

> What a Friend we have in Jesus,
> All our sins and griefs to bear!

What a privilege to carry
Everything to God in prayer!
O what *peace* we often forfeit,
O what needless pain we bear,
All because we do not carry
Everything to God in prayer!

Have we trials and temptations?
Is there trouble anywhere?
We should never be discouraged,
Take it to the Lord in prayer.
Can we find a Friend so faithful
Who will all our sorrows share?
Jesus knows our every weakness,
Take it to the Lord in prayer.

Are we weak and heavy laden,
Cumbered with a load of care?
Precious Saviour, still our refuge—
Take it to the Lord in prayer.
Do thy friends despise, forsake thee?
Take it to the Lord in prayer;
In His arms He'll take and shield thee,
Thou wilt find a solace there.

A Corporate Experience

It is important to emphasize that prayer, though it should be a *personal* ongoing experience, should also be *corporate*. We are to pray for one another. If any one thing comes clear in the Book of Acts and in the letters written to the churches, it is that each of us needs other members of the body of Christ. We need to be involved in regular prayer experiences with other Christians.

I learned this lesson very clearly one day. Several circumstances in my ministry were causing a lot of anxiety. In fact, after sleeping a few short hours one night, I awakened and spent the rest of the night tossing and turning. Since I was scheduled to attend a men's early morning prayer meeting, my alarm went off at 5 A.M.—a couple of hours after I had already awakened.

Interestingly, this happened the very week that I was preparing this material on Paul's words to the Philippians. Consequently, I was motivated to pray about my problems. But in all honesty, I felt very little relief from the emotional stress. Incidentally, I have often found that when I am preparing a message on a particular theme, the Lord seemingly allows me to experience some of the same things I am studying about. The Lord knows how to keep a pastor honest.

When I got up that morning, I dressed and headed for the prayer session. While sitting with those men, praying—not about my own anxiety and concerns, but about other people's problems—the anxiety suddenly lifted from my heart. Somehow I knew that God was going to work everything out. And He did!

I learned that God honors corporate prayer. In my case, I found inner peace just participating in corporate prayer. How much more so will this process work when we also pray together about these things that are causing anxiety?

A Challenge

1. List the major source of your anxiety at this moment in your life:

_____

_____

2. Pray and thank God for:
   • Your eternal salvation.
   • The unique privilege of prayer.
   • God's Word and His promises.
   Who shall separate us from the love of Christ? Shall trouble or hardship or persecution or famine or naked-

ness or danger or sword? . . . No, in all these things we are more than conquerors through Him who loved us. For I am convinced that neither death nor life, neither angels nor demons, neither the present nor the future, nor any powers, neither height nor depth, nor anything else in all creation, will be able to separate us from the love of God that is in Christ Jesus our Lord (Rom. 8:35, 37-39).

• Your brothers and sisters in Christ.

3. Tell God how much you love Him. Demonstrate that love by praying the following prayer (a paraphrase of Rom. 12:1-2):

Dear Father, in view of Your marvelous love and grace in giving Your Son to die for me, I now offer You my body as a living sacrifice, holy and pleasing to You—which is my spiritual worship. I will no longer conform my life to the pattern of this world, but I will be transformed by the renewing of my mind. I realize that I will then be able to test and approve what Your will is—Your good, perfect, and pleasing will.

4. Ask God to meet your need in His own way and time.

5. Share this need with several other committed Christians so they can pray for you.

6. Join or organize a small prayer group where you can regularly praise God and pray for one another.

Father, in the midst of circumstances that create anxiety—whether it be my material needs, my daily responsibilities, or criticism from those who oppose my Christian beliefs—help me to pray about everything. I thank You first of all for my salvation, the privilege of prayer, God's promises in the Scriptures, and my brothers and sisters in Christ. Now help me to trust you to meet my needs in Your own way and time.

A Project

Invite several of your close Christian friends to join you in studying this chapter. Ask them if they are interested in forming a small prayer group.

12
A Final Perspective

Since Paul wrote more letters to first-century churches than any other New Testament author, it is logical to conclude that his writings provide us with numerous references to prayer, both by way of example and exhortation. Let's look at two more of those examples and a final exhortation.

Paul's Focus on Thanksgiving
When Christians pray, they should always do so "with thanksgiving." This was Paul's constant emphasis. No matter what our problems, concerns, or mental and emotional states, true believers can develop a focus beyond themselves. That focus is a spirit of thanksgiving, not only for what God has done for us personally in providing us with eternal hope and everlasting life, but for our relationships with other members of the body of Christ.

The Ephesians
Paul beautifully exemplifies this attitude of thanksgiving in his prayer for the Ephesians. When he heard of their faith in Christ and their love for others, he stated, "I have not stopped *giving thanks for you,* remembering you in my prayers" (Eph. 1:16).

The appreciation for other Christians expressed in this prayer

124

becomes more meaningful when we understand the context in which it was written. Paul was in a Roman prison. Though he had freedom to write and interact with those who came to see him (Acts 28:30), the missionary activity that had characterized his life was severely thwarted.

Though restricted physically, Paul was certainly not restricted mentally. Not only did he use his time to share Christ with the Roman guards and those who came to see him, but he also spent many hours thinking and writing, and above all—praying.

Paul's mental reflections and prayers were intermingled, for in those lonely hours, his mind went back to those believers he had led to Christ and nurtured in the faith. Again and again he thanked God for his Christian brothers and sisters—not only because they were growing in Christ, but because of what they meant to him personally.

The Philippians

Paul's appreciation for other believers is more obvious in his Philippian letter than in any other. From a Roman prison he wrote:

> I *thank my God* every time I remember you. In all my
> prayers for all of you, I always pray with joy because
> of your partnership in the Gospel from the first day
> until now, being confident of this, that He who began
> a good work in you will carry it on to completion until
> the day of Christ Jesus.
>
> It is right for me to feel this way about all of you, since
> I have you in my heart; whether I am in chains or
> defending and confirming the Gospel, all of you share
> in God's grace with me (Phil. 1:3-7).

The *partnership in the Gospel* Paul wrote about here is very concrete and practical. He later elaborated. Hearing he was in prison, the Philippians had sent Paul a gift—probably food, clothing, and money. He concluded his letter by saying, "I rejoice greatly in the Lord that at last you have renewed your concern for me" (4:10). Being human he probably wondered if they had forgotten him. But when Epaphroditus appeared with their gifts of love, Paul was overwhelmed with joy and appreciation.

He reminded them that from the beginning of their relationship in Christ, no church had cared for him personally and had been as generous as they had. Thus we understand more fully why they had a special place in his heart (1:7), and why he began his letter, "I thank my God every time I remember you. In all my prayers for all of you, I always pray with joy" (vv. 3-4).

Philemon

Paul not only "thanked God" for *groups* of Christians—as illustrated in his prison letters written to the Ephesians, Philippians, and Colossians (Col. 1:3)—but he also focused his prayers of thanksgiving on particular individuals. This is most clearly illustrated in his letter to Philemon. Again, writing from a Roman prison, he stated:

> I always *thank my God* as I remember you in my prayers because I hear about your faith in the Lord Jesus and your love for all the saints. I pray that you may be active in sharing your faith, so that you'll have a full understanding of every good thing we have in Christ. Your love has given me great joy and encouragement, because you, brother, have refreshed the hearts of the saints (Phile. 4—7).

Paul had an unusual relationship with Philemon, a well-to-do businessman who lived in Colossae. Paul had led this man to Christ and often stayed in his home during his missionary travels.

Later, one of Philemon's servants, a man named Onesimus, took advantage of the new freedom Philemon gave his slaves following his conversion. He stole some goods and money and headed off for Rome, probably attempting to maintain anonymity in the crowds in that great city. Evidently Onesimus got in trouble with Roman authorities and ended up in the same prison as Paul, who recognized him and led him to Christ.

When Onesimus was released from prison, Paul sent him

back to Colossae with a short letter—the letter identified in the New Testament as *Philemon*. It's a brief letter but rich in content, reflecting Paul's deep appreciation for this man. Thus, he began the letter, "I *always thank my God* as I remember you in my prayers" (1:4).

The prison epistles particularly focus on Paul's spirit of thankfulness and deep appreciation for other Christians. Though his relationship with God in Jesus Christ was more important than any other, it was his friends in Christ who provided that warm, secure feeling that we all need in times of difficulty and stress.

Paul's Prayer Requests

If you were in prison because of your faith in Christ and you were writing a letter to your friends, what would you ask them to pray about? Again, Paul models for us a spirit of selflessness that is—outside of Christ's example—unmatched in Christian history.

In his letter to the Ephesians he requested prayer, not for himself and his own physical and emotional needs—but for *boldness* to communicate the message of Christ. "Pray also for me," he wrote, "that whenever I open my mouth, words may be given me so that I will fearlessly make known the mystery of the Gospel, for which I am an ambassador in chains. Pray that I may declare it fearlessly, as I should" (Eph. 6:19-20).

Paul's letter to the Colossians focuses on the same concern. "Devote yourselves to prayer, being watchful and *thankful*. And pray for us, too, that God *may open a door for our message,* so we may proclaim the mystery of Christ, for which I am in chains. Pray that I may proclaim it *clearly* as I should" (Col. 4:2-4).

If most of us were in Paul's situation, we'd probably be praying for protection, or release, or that our personal needs would be met. This would not be wrong—for us or Paul. But these concerns were not the focus of Paul's personal prayers. Rather, he prayed for boldness to proclaim the message of Christ and for the ability to proclaim that message clearly. What an example of unselfishness in prayer!

Paul's Special Exhortation

The focus of this series has been on mutual prayer concern among believers and this is as it should be. Paul, especially, exhorted believers to get beyond themselves in their prayer concerns and interests. This is also the thrust of his opening remarks in 1 Timothy 2. These remarks are particularly relevant because they involve specific instructions regarding what Christians should pray for when they gather to worship the Lord. Paul wrote, "I urge, then, *first of all,* that requests, prayers, intercession, and thanksgiving be made for everyone" (1 Tim. 2:1).

This kind of praying should be a priority. It should be "first of all." It is my hope that we will remember to pray for "everyone"—not just ourselves.

Note too that Paul is very specific regarding *who* we should pray for. The word *everyone* includes "kings and all those in authority." This is particularly significant since political and religious leaders in Paul's day were often hostile to the Gospel of Christ. That, of course, is why he was in prison.

Consequently, Paul was not only exhorting, but also *exemplifying.* If any man had a right to be angry and hostile toward his persecutors, Paul did. But his respect and concern for government authorities—pagan though they were—is an example to us all. Though he did not compromise his Christian convictions—which eventually caused his death—he never allowed himself to be disrespectful to authority figures. Thus he wrote to the Roman Christians, "Everyone must submit himself to the governing authorities, for there is no authority except that which God has established" (Rom. 13:1).

Paul's exhortation to pray for government leaders, however, had far deeper meaning than just praying for these leaders' personal welfare. His primary concern was that Christians would "live peaceful and quiet lives in all godliness and holiness" (1 Tim. 2:2). Persecution was already rampant and to further rebel against the government would only bring more persecution.

But Paul's prayer goes even further. Why pray for government leaders in order that we might live peaceful and quiet lives? Paul once again brings into clear focus one of the most important reasons God has left His children on this earth— "This is good," Paul wrote, "and pleases God our Saviour, who wants all men to be saved and come to the knowledge of the truth" (vv. 3-4).

A peaceful and quiet environment, free from persecution, allows Christians to live godly lives, demonstrating and modeling the reality of Christianity. It provides opportunities to communicate the Good News of Jesus Christ to all people so that they might respond to the Gospel and enter into eternal life. Paul makes it clear that Jesus Christ is the only One who can provide that eternal life. Thus he adds, "For there is one God and one Mediator between God and men, the man Christ Jesus, who gave Himself a ransom for all men" (vv. 5-6).

Persecution and repression have often caused Christians to intensify their witness for Christ and to stand boldly for what they believe. But Christianity spreads much more rapidly in an environment of freedom.

All of us were encouraged and amazed at what happened during the years of repression in Red China. It is estimated that in spite of intense persecution, Chinese believers increased from 800,000 to nearly 4 million.

Without missionaries, without Bibles, without strong leadership, they multiplied—quoting Scripture from memory, copying Scriptures from radio broadcasts beamed into China, and meeting in secret.

But think what is happening now that the doors are opening. There are nearly 1 billion Chinese people representing 25 percent of the world's population. Those in the research department of Christian Communications, Limited in Hong Kong estimate that less than 1 percent of these people are true believers! If this new freedom continues, many more than ever before will find Jesus Christ as personal Saviour. This is the burden of Paul's exhortation to Timothy.

Some Final Questions

1. What is the focus of your prayers?

Paul's initial focus was thanksgiving—thankfulness to God for others. What about you and me? How easy it is to forget about what others mean to us, how we got where we are, and why we're doing what we're doing. Most of us are deeply indebted to others for whatever success we may be enjoying in life—our parents, our mates, our business associates, our former teachers—and in many instances, our children.

When I was writing this chapter, I received a call from a man living in Wheaton, Illinois. Both my wife and I knew what he was going to say the moment we heard his voice. A very special mutual friend had gone home to be with the Lord.

I have referred to this man before in my messages and books. He was a former professor of mine at Moody Bible Institute named Harold Garner. This man took an interest in me as a student when I was theologically and emotionally confused. He believed in me when I didn't believe in myself. He became a second father to me when my own father, supportive as he was, did not have the theological and experiential resources to help me ferret out the answers to my deep questions. Later, Dr. Garner and his wife introduced me to Elaine, whom I later married—a great contribution to my life!

When I received word of his death, I was not surprised, for he had suffered from heart disease for many years. I did not feel badly about his death, for I knew where he was—with Jesus Christ. I *did* feel badly, however, that I had not followed through on something I had planned to do for some time.

Ever since my book *Encouraging One Another* had been published, I planned to send Dr. Garner a special autographed copy, because I had used him as an illustration several times in the book. To me, he had been a real encourager—a 20th-century Barnabas. My regrets were that I had waited too long. This unique opportunity to encourage him had passed me by. Though I have remembered him in special ways over the years, I could have done better—especially since he meant so much to me.

What about you? Have you forgotten people who have meant a lot to you? Do you thank God for them and let them know, as Paul did, that you *are* thanking God for them?

2. What kinds of requests dominate your prayer life?

In the midst of difficulties, even persecution and suffering, Paul's prayers focused on his great calling in life—to help others find Christ and grow in the faith. Not that he did not pray about his own needs, but his focus was on God and others.

When someone asks you what they can pray for in your life, how do you respond? How often do you request prayer that you can be a better witness for Christ? A better example to your children? A better Christian wife or husband? Or a more effective Christian? We should, if we follow Paul's example (1 Cor. 11:1).

3. How much do you pray for government officials?

Paul clearly teaches that this should be a priority in the church. In America, it's easy to take our freedom for granted— for we've always known freedom. This does not excuse us from praying for our government leaders. We must remember that what we have may not always be. Let us continually thank God for our open and free society, but let us pray that this freedom will not destroy us. Moral decay and unethical behavior is eating away at the foundations of our society. If ever prayer for government officials was needed, it's now!

A Challenge

Evaluate the structure of your prayers in view of Paul's example and exhortations.

First, in your prayers, thank God regularly for other Christians who have impacted your life. Then, following Paul's example, tell them that you are thanking God for them.

Second, establish priorities in your prayer requests. Pray regularly that God will use you to communicate His message of love to others. Then pray about your own personal needs.

Third, pray regularly for government officials—at the national, state, and local levels. Pray that these leaders will help create an environment that will allow us to lead peaceful lives in our society, enabling us to practice our faith and Christian lifestyle freely. Pray that the results of our prayers and our lifestyle will lead to the salvation of many—both those who are leading us, and all people. Note: This life response can be applied both corporately and personally.

> *Father, I thank You for those Christians who have impacted my life in a special way* (here include some names). *I thank You for those who are encouraging me regularly, especially my pastor, the other leaders in my church, and the other members of my local church.*
>
> *Help me to communicate Your message of love to all people. Forgive me for praying so selfishly and forgetting to focus on others first.*
>
> *Father, I also pray for the President of the United States, and all state and local government officials. Give them wisdom to make decisions that will protect our free society from decay and corruption. May we always have a peaceful environment in which to communicate Your message of salvation clearly, both in our lifestyle and in what we say.*

A Project

Now that you have completed this book, establish a study group to study these chapters together. If you have already studied the book in a group, consider starting your own group and repeat the process for others. If you have any questions and/or comments, please feel free to write me personally at the following address:

DR. GENE A. GETZ
BIBLICAL CENTER FOR CHURCH RENEWAL
200 CHISHOLM PLACE, SUITE 228
PLANO, TEXAS 75075